DAVE DICKSON:

THE STORY SO FA

Dave Dickson was born some time ago but does not remember much about it, apart from 'someone hitting me'.

Later he went to school and later still, for want of anything better to do, he became a journalist. This meant he could sleep in the morning and stay awake all night. And get paid for it. In the course of his career he has received cheques from *Kerrang!*, *Metal Hammer*, *Record Mirror*, *Raw*, of which he was one of the founders, *Rolling Stone* and a bunch of other Japanese, European and American mags whose names he cannot recall. He also contributes to *Cosmic World* and has even been published by *Knave*.

He has jetted around the world at other people's expense and met a lot of famous people including the coolest man in rock 'n' roll, Keith Richards, of whom he asked, 'You got any Jack Daniel's?'

He collects comics for a hobby, reads Gore Vidal for pleasure and listens to the Rolling Stones and the Sisters of Mercy for recreation.

BIOGRAPHIZE

—— THE ——
DEF LEPPARD
STORY

DAVE DICKSON

PAN BOOKS

First published 1995 by Sidgwick & Jackson Ltd

This edition published 1996 by Pan Books
an imprint of Macmillan General Books
25 Eccleston Place
London SW1W 9NF
and Basingstoke

Associated companies throughout the world

ISBN 0 330 34693 8

A CIP catalogue record for this book is available from
the British Library.

Typeset by CentraCet Limited, Cambridge
Printed and bound in Great Britain

CONTENTS

ACKNOWLEDGEMENTS

There are various people I would like to thank who, in one way or another, knowingly or unknowingly, contributed to the writing of this book. So, my heartfelt thanks to: Geoff Banks; Dante Bonutto; Frank Stuart-Brown; Jane Chapman; Mark Crampton; Malcolm Dome; Geoff Gillespie; Janice Issitt; Ida Langsam; Ché Osborne; Jem Reeve; *Riff Raff* magazine; Val Rooker; Mick Wall; and Mark Woodley.

And a special thanks to Joe Mackett, without whose help, advice, diligence and investigative skills you would not now be holding this biography.

This book is for Neil, because I owe you;
and for Chris, because I never forget.

CHAPTER ONE

BORN TO BOOGIE

Joe Elliott was a tall, sturdy lad, broad shouldered and fair haired. He looked like a typical steel-mill apprentice. There were thousands like him in Sheffield, northern England, brought up in a generation of plenty suddenly cast out into a world where there was nothing. Nothing except the steel mills, a few connected industries . . . or the dole queue. But Joe was different; Joe wasn't of the same stock as those thousands of others. Because Joe had a dream. The dream, in those tentative years, was called Deaf Leopard and it was a rock 'n' roll band that, one day, would lead him to superstardom.

Sheffield is a bleak, grey city that appears to be constantly damp. To the unwary traveller passing through its streets just after it has rained the impression is of a city where it has *always* rained and always will rain. It has a grim and melancholy feel to it accentuated by its steep, narrow streets. Its walls and its streets are grey, even its skies are often grey. Greyness seems a way of life in Sheffield.

Sheffield is too much city crammed into too small a space. It is situated at the confluence of two rivers, the Sheaf and the Don, in what was once (and by the residents still is) known as the West Riding district of Yorkshire. But then government boundary changes put paid to all that sort of poetic nonsense. Positioned at the foothills of the eastern slopes of the Pennine range (often referred to as the backbone of England), Sheffield folk are a tough and hardy people, typical of their native Yorkshire.

Yorkshire itself is famous for numerous qualities, not least its broad dialect and its bitter, the local beer. Its populatoin is fanatical in its love of cricket and, to a lesser extent, rugby and soccer. And they have a fierce pride in being Yorkshiremen. They are a tough people born into a tough and occasionally barren and inhospitable landscape.

Sheffield, though, has one particular commodity for which it is famous the world over: steel. Much of the metropolis's citizens are given over to the manufacture of high-quality steel and its by-products, in particular cutlery and tools. It was towards Sheffield's grim, and perhaps Satanic and rather oppressive steel mills that most kids of Joe's generation were headed, if they were lucky to get that far.

In the post-war years Sheffield underwent an extensive urban redevelopment programme with much of the city centre being completely reshaped and rebuilt under the auspices of a socially conscious local council, which also developed a major housing scheme taking advantage of the hilly nature of the city's site, attempting to graft on an entirely new image for the rather Dickensian city.

To a degree they succeeded, but none of this imaginative rebuilding could alter the fact that Sheffield was a city dedicated to heavy industry, and when the world economic depression took root around the mid-1970s it was just such cities as Sheffield that bore the heaviest brunt of its assault. Sure, Sheffield boasted its own university, but this was beyond the reach of the vast majority of kids approaching their last days of school as factories closed and having a job looked like becoming the exception rather than the rule.

Given this kind of social environment, coupled with the inherent toughness of the Yorkshire people, it is little wonder that the style of music most beloved by many of Sheffield's youth was of a similarly hard, tough, and gritty style: rock. And the particular type of rock music most favoured has been given an assortment of names: Heavy Metal, Heavy Rock, Hard Rock – but essentially it was rock 'n' roll played with plenty of power and plenty of aggression. There are numerous reasons – if any sociologist ever took time out to investigate them – why the industrial areas of Britain should be such a particularly strong breeding ground for bands given to this type of music. Birmingham, the heart of Britain's industrial Midlands, has spawned and nurtured two of the archetypal Heavy Metal bands of the late 1960s and early '70s, Black Sabbath and Led Zeppelin, and later Judas Priest. Similarly, it was no geographical coincidence that two of the major forces of the New Wave of British Heavy Metal, as it became known, that emerged from the punk era came from two northern industrial towns mere miles apart. Saxon were based in Barnsley and, just a few miles to the south, Sheffield offered up a band called Def Leppard. The pragmatic, no-nonsense, hard-edged people of Yorkshire are naturally enamoured of a similar style of music.

Far away from London, the home of both the music industry and its attendant media, the kids themselves tend to be that much *less* influenced by the fads and fashions that spring up and fall down again as quickly on the streets of the capital. Being 'hip' doesn't have quite the same all-important *cachet* in Sheffield as it does in London.

None the less, to escape the rut that was being created around them, and entirely beyond their control, there remained two plausible options open to a young and ambitious Sheffield kid. The first was to become a professional footballer. Sheffield boasted two soccer teams, Sheffield Wednesday and Sheffield United. But, whatever modicum of success the clubs could obtain on the field, they were not 'glamour' teams like Liverpool or Manchester United or some of their London rivals. While the players might be local heroes they were not destined to be anything other than bit-players on the world stage. Besides which, Joe knew he wanted a big slice of that second option, that second escape route. And he'd wanted it as long as he could remember: he wanted to be a pop star!

In art classes at school Joe would spend his time designing posters featuring his dream band playing the Sheffield City Hall – *the* pinnacle of achievement as far as Sheffield was concerned – Deaf Leopard! The band's logo would be some approximation of a leopard clutching an old-fashioned ear-trumpet to the side of its head. It was, in effect, a spoof of the famous 'Nipper' HMV emblem. And instead of writing the prescribed essays in English lessons the young Elliott would script rave concert reviews of a non-existent band called Deaf Leopard. Quizzed by his teachers as to precisely what kind of career he intended to pursue when he left school, Joe would invariably reply: 'I want to be a pop star!' Unfortunately, his careers advisers could find no suitable course listed on their files. There was clearly no help to be gleaned from that quarter.

Neither was Joe alone in this peculiar unclassified, filed, stapled, or mutilated dream.

Tapton Comprehensive seems an unlikely launching pad for one of the world's most successful rock bands. But it was here that future Def Leppard bassist Rick Savage and original guitarist Pete Willis met up to discover they shared a common goal: they wanted to be rock 'n' rollers!

The Comprehensive School system was introduced in Britain by the Labour government in the idealistic '60s with the express intention of giving every child an equal opportunity to achieve the best grades and best opportunities for further education, doing away with the previous two-tier system where the smart kids went to Grammar Schools and everyone else went to Secondary Moderns. As high-minded and noble as this scheme seemed it was inevitably doomed to failure. By having exclusively mixed-ability classes throughout the school system it simply meant that the pace of learning was bound to be set by the slower members of the class. And for kids with dreams, especially those of becoming pop stars, it didn't offer much incentive.

For smarter kids like Rick and Pete this whole idea simply meant hours of terminal boredom locked into a system that was intended to benefit them. Instead they turned inward and relied on themselves to relieve the drudgery of school life. And turning to their own resources meant turning to music.

In those days Rick (nicknamed Sav) was a guitar player like Pete and together, at the tender age of fourteen, they decided to form the nucleus of a band that was eventually to become Def Leppard. They would skip classes to rehearse their set – in those formative days basically a greatest hits collection of old Deep Purple numbers together with more poppy numbers stolen from the back catalogues of such bands as T-Rex, Thin Lizzy, and Mott The Hoople.

Eventually the paths of Messrs Elliott, Savage, and Willis would cross when Atomic Mass, as Sav had dubbed his initial group, dispensed with their singer. The band members persuaded Joe in to front the act because 'he looked the part'. Previously Joe had never sung, he'd only played guitar and drummed in an assortment of garage bands. But Atomic Mass wanted a singer – so Joe Elliott became a singer.

And the new singer brought with him more than his presence and force of personality. He also brought along the moniker of his dream band, Deaf Leopard. And so, with the recruitment of the new – in every sense of the word – vocalist, Atomic Mass was dropped in favour of the Elliott vision, which itself went through some minor mutations and ultimately emerged as *Def Leppard*.

A band, of sorts, was born, and the three Sheffield kids who shared a common dream of success had taken their first tentative steps along the path to fame and fortune.

CHAPTER TWO

ROCK PRETTY BABY

With the nucleus of the band formed, the skeleton of Elliott, Savage, and Willis now required some flesh. There had never been any doubt in their minds what *type* of band Def Leppard was going to be. It was in their blood, as deeply ingrained as any of the Yorkshiremen's natural inclinations – Yorkshire bitter, black pudding, cricket: they were going to be a Heavy Metal band, no question.

Despite the prevailing winds of musical fashion which blew with no little fury both against the band and what they held dear – at the time Britain was swinging from the death throes of the punk movement toward the feyness of the New Romantics – there could be no wavering from the cause. Def Leppard would weather the storm and become a Heavy Metal band and that was that.

The important difference at this stage – and something that would eventually set Def Leppard aside from the rest of the pack and ensure their phenomenal success both in the US and across most of the world – was that there were diverse elements to their collective listening habits. Together they explored shades and nuances that simply weren't present, at least to the same degree, amongst their contemporaries in what would become known as the New Wave of British Heavy Metal. At its simplest,

Def Leppard took from their earliest influences a sense of melody, almost 'popism', that was to infuse their own compositions with as much *danceability* as pure power. They were never simple riff merchants, their songs were to take on all the best elements of mainstream pop – the singalong choruses, the memorable melodies – and couple them with the power and sheer aggressive force of the classic Heavy Metal bands.

Even the most cursory glance down the list of these early major influences shows how soon they were to appreciate the importance of a simple hook line and a good tune. They veered away from the archetypal 'headbanging' Heavy Metal bands and more toward those whose songs contained the same melodic structure that came to define Leppard's own work: the likes of Thin Lizzy, UFO, and Led Zeppelin. (Indeed, some critics have even argued that the very name *Def Leppard* was in fact ripped off from Led Zeppelin, claiming that it *subliminally* reminded the fan of the '70s supergroup. Others might suggest this was stretching elementary psychology to its very extremes and beyond! Whatever reasons Joe Elliott had for concocting the title in the first place, aping Led Zeppelin's name cannot, surely, have been at the forefront. But, like Lead Zeppelin becoming Led Zeppelin – they didn't want anyone mispronouncing the name – Deaf Leopard mutated into Def Leppard for reasons now lost to obscurity.) These groups all took great pains largely to dissociate themselves from the bulk of Heavy Metal bands, concluding that the term 'Heavy Metal' itself was rather degrading and limiting – considering some of the bands that did stand proudly under that banner, you could see their point – and certainly it detracted from the rather more elaborate and often subtle, even occasionally *classically* based material they were recording. They did not welcome their pigeon-holing in the Heavy Metal bracket and neither, consequently, did Def Leppard, preferring such looser categories as Hard Rock, or just plain Rock 'n' Roll.

But by whatever standard they operated, there was no doubting the essential *heavyness* of Def Leppard's music. However, over that foundation they began to add the shading of those other influences, acts such as T-Rex, David Bowie, and Mott The Hoople. This combination brought to their music a unique texture until a picture was built up of songs that were basically heavy – certainly heavy enough for the hard-core rock fans – but with the added ingredient of a certain pop sensibility. Clearly, with the kind of influences Def Leppard numbered early in their career their own material, when it began to see the light of day and the feel of guitar string, was somewhat out of the ordinary. Although much of their earliest work was, understand-ably, very derivative it at least showed the promise of young musicians who possessed that all too indefinable something extra. Their songs, if nothing else, seemed destined to take them to stardom!

So, with their musical direction at least clear from the outset the trio needed to find themselves some like-minded compatriots to swell the ranks of Def Leppard into a fully fledged group.

Steve Clark had a certain physical resemblance to Pete Willis. Both were rather slight, almost frail figures who looked far from set on a course bound for rock 'n' roll stardom. Clark was thin and rakish, his spindly frame topped by a mass of blond, curly hair. Pete was slightly shorter, more stocky, and possessed a set of full-blooded lips that gave him an appearance not dissimilar to Aerosmith singer Steve Tyler. But both Steve and Pete had a certain 'pinched' look about their faces, a kind of struggling artist, almost anaemic quality that somehow managed to couple a kind of mean and hungry street-wise look with that of two lost boys who needed to be mothered.

Aside from this casual physical similarity they also both played guitar, although neither was aware of the fact prior to their first meeting. And that fateful event took place because of a third affinity, amongst a mounting series: they both attended the same day-release class at a local college of further education.

Steve spotted Pete reading a guitar manual and instantly realized they were kindred spirits, at least as far as their choice of musical instrument was concerned. Where Pete had the edge on Steve was that he had a band. While this initial crossing of paths might have come to nothing, the seeds were sown so that when they came together again, some while later, a fruitful relationship could begin in earnest.

The next time the two met, then, was in the slightly more convivial surroundings of Sheffield's City Hall. It was here, in this rather ornate and beautiful stone edifice, that kids such as Pete and Steve would come to flee from the tedium of their otherwise drab and grey existence, where they could put up barricades against the onrush of the scornful, cynical punk movement as they came together with other like-minded devotees to listen to their favourite Heavy Metal bands and enjoy a couple of hours of pure escapism. Here was where the Sheffield Hard Rock fans came to get their rocks off!

That particular night the visiting Heavy Metal Heroes were the new kings of Birmingham Heavy Metal, Judas Priest. Birmingham stood for many years as *the* home of British – and consequently world – Heavy Metal. Following in the footsteps of Sabbath and Zeppelin, Judas Priest were carrying the torch for Birmingham. It wasn't until Def Leppard themselves began to emerge that Birmingham's place at the centre of the maelstrom actually began to be challenged. But that night it was the 'Brummies', Judas Priest, who held court in Sheffield. And their visit provided not only entertainment for the collected hordes of denim-clad Metal fans, it also accounted for the second and most significant meeting between the two guitarists.

Pete and Steve quickly fell into conversation, recognizing now that they shared a love not only for the same instrument but also for the effect to which that instrument could be put. And Def Leppard were on the look-out for kindred spirits and Pete certainly found just that in Steve.

Pete explained about the band and invited Steve along to one of their rehearsal sessions. Of such chance meetings are rock 'n' roll legends often born and this was to be no exception. Steve took Pete up on the invitation and showed up. He was suitably impressed with what he saw and what he heard, and the feeling from Pete Willis and Co. was quite mutual. A pact was formed and Def Leppard from that point onward became a twin-guitar band and could start work on creating and refining a sound that was truly their own.

With the posts of singer and guitarist now filled, Rick Savage having moved from guitar to bass to make way for Steve, only the drum stool remained without a permanent fixture. Def Leppard went through an assortment of different drummers. Of these, the most notable were Frank Noon, who drummed on the classic and ground-breaking *Getcha Rocks Off* EP and later went on to join other 'New Wave' Heavy Metal acts such as Lionheart, Stampede, and Waystead alongside former UFO bassist Pete Way, and Tony Kenning, who occupied the Def Leppard drum stool prior to being replaced by the band's permanent skin-beater Rick Allen.

Rick's entry into the ranks of Def Leppard has something of the fairy-tale to it. Rick had been playing in bands since he was ten with a string of unlikely acts with equally unlikely names; Smokey Blue was one such. Then one day he saw a newspaper advert that caught his eye and piqued his interest. It read: 'Leopard loses skin' – Def Leppard were still Deaf Leopard at this point – which proved to be the band's rather obtuse way of advertising for a replacement drummer, Mr Kenning having departed. Rick went along, passed the audition, and the Leopard could thereafter boast a new skin. Only this time it was permanent.

In these formative post-school days, times were lean for any aspiring musician but particularly for a band who were playing music that most people of any influence would have considered out-dated and out-moded. After all, wasn't the whole point of the punk movement, to kill off the dinosaurs of the Heavy Metal age?

At the time record companies were engaged in a weird and peculiarly paranoid frenzy of deal-signings. Anyone and anything, so long as it was punk, was being snapped up regardless of their musical or artistic merits (or lack of them in most cases).

The Svengali of the punk movement, Sex Pistols manager Malcolm McLaren, rode this wave for all it was worth and presided over a veritable orgy of A&R hype. The A&R men – A&R stands for 'Artists & Repertoire', the people in the record companies who actually sign new acts to the company roster; in fact it's a typically self-important music biz term for 'talent scout' – paid court to McLaren and his protégés. And McLaren, for his part, lapped it up, gleaning hundreds of thousands of pounds from both EMI and A&M Records in their eagerness to snap up the band before they ever had any real idea what they were getting themselves into. All they knew for sure was the fact that the Pistols were a punk band – some might argue they were *the* punk band – and everyone told them, the music press, the clubs, informed DJs, that punk was 'in', that it was 'happening', and would prove to be very big business. So, since nobody wanted to be left out when the party began, the record companies started to panic when the press began to rave about this new movement and they were suddenly forced to admit they hadn't got a clue what was going on. Frightening stuff. So, if you were a punk band in 1978 and you looked the part and could talk your way in front of some record company A&R men, chances are you'd get signed. After all, not since the days of the Merseybeat and the frantic search for 'the new Beatles' had so much pressure been applied to so few men with so little real knowledge of what was actually happening on the music scene. Now, suddenly, they had to find 'the new Damned/Clash/Sex Pistols', and consequently signed up a lot of pale imitation junk. This, then, was the prevailing atmosphere into which Def Leppard were cast.

The problem Def Leppard faced in 1978, still as Deaf Leopard, was that they *weren't* a punk band. They didn't even look like one and, consequently, there was *absolutely no* possibility of getting themselves in front of an A&R man. And even if they had they certainly weren't what the A&R men had been told to go out and find: they had long hair, they could play their instruments, and they played songs by bands like Deep Purple and Thin Lizzy, and wasn't that *exactly* what everybody was supposed to be rebelling against? If times were lean for aspiring musicians in 1978, times were all but destitute for Def Leppard with their advocacy of Hard Rock and wanting to be able to play properly and other such ludicrous flights of young fancy.

But Def Leppard knew what they wanted, and what they wanted was to be a Hard Rock band. 'We just wanted to be big in Sheffield!' admitted Sav later. That was all, a little local renown for doing what they did best. What they didn't really know then was how to go about getting it; but all that was to begin falling into place before long.

The young cubs of Def Leppard rehearsed in a solitary room in an old building close to Sheffield United Football Club. The use of this hovel cost them the princely sum of £5 a week. By this time Messrs Elliott, Savage, Willis and Clark had all left school – some had even found jobs! – while the as yet undiscovered Rick, some three to four years younger than the rest of the band, was still slaving over his lessons. Joe drove a van around the streets of Sheffield delivering machine parts, while Sav worked for British Rail. Only Steve found himself engaged in Sheffield's prime industrial activity, steel, as a lathe worker. Meanwhile, some fifty miles south of Sheffield, a lad by the name of Phil Collen was learning how to be an electrician.

On Friday afternoons, after work, the four, plus whoever was the current drummer, would rendezvous at their £5-a-week rehearsal 'studio' and practise their craft. At the time their repertoire was rather limited featuring only material plundered from a back catalogue of 'greatest hits' by their heroes. They played Thin Lizzy numbers when Pete and Steve realized they could accurately reproduce Lizzy's twin-lead guitar-harmonies instead of simply playing one as a lead instrument and the other as an additional part of the rhythm section as was usually the case in two-guitar bands. With this rather stunning revelation they managed to introduce yet another Lizzy classic, 'Emerald', to their ever expanding set-list of covers.

They had also made their own first tentative steps into the

field of composition. Joe took up the reins of lyricist leaving the riff-writing to Sav and Pete. Their first efforts were clumsy, even embarrassing copies of older, more familiar Heavy Metal standards, but they were trying. One of their better attempts was a number called 'Misty Dreamer', which later had its title changed to 'Sorrow Is A Woman' before it made its appearance on Leppard's début album, *On Through The Night*, some two years later. But while their songwriting talents developed they were still very much a 'cover' band.

Their Friday night rehearsals would frequently take them way past midnight and into the small hours of the morning, often until 4 a.m. But, in truth, this was nothing more than a measure of their obsessive dedication to their art. They wanted to be able to play properly, together, and in time, while all around them bands were springing up who barely knew one end of a guitar from the other. One famous punk anthem of the time was the Adverts' 'One Chord Wonders'. But that kind of anarchic, slipshod attitude simply didn't hold water with Def Leppard. They wanted to create *music*, not noise; so they rehearsed.

Eventually they got to the stage where they were rehearsing for up to four hours a night, every night during the week, often spilling over into the weekends as Steve and Pete developed the style that was shortly to set them apart as obvious leaders of the 'New Wave of British Heavy Metal' pack. Indeed, this minute attention to the details of their actual playing at such an early stage may well be the reason for the Leppard's ultimate success. That they had the professionalism to recognize the importance of being able to play well so early in their career stood them in good stead when their big break eventually came.

What marked Def Leppard out as being that extra bit different from the other runners in the pack was, firstly, their songs and their obvious songwriting talents; and secondly, the fact that they really could play their instruments, even though they were still remarkably young and inexperienced and especially at a time when *not* being able to play correctly seemed almost a positive virtue. When they hit the stage – even though these stages were small, dingy, and clearly unfit for the purpose to which they were being put in those days – they hit it as though it were a major stadium they were playing and not merely some local pub or working men's club. They brought with them a remarkably professional attitude and approach when 'amateurism' seemed very much the order of the day. Although being 'big in Sheffield' was their only avowed aim it was clear that deep in the back of their minds there lurked some rather grander ambitions. Some may have called them 'delusions of grandeur' but those delusions were, before very long, to turn into hard and fast reality.

With enough rehearsal time under their collective belts they put themselves to the ultimate test for the first time in July 1978: Def Leppard played their first ever gig.

The venue for this historic occasion was Westfield School in Sheffield and it was, perhaps, a less than auspicious start to their career proper. However, they still managed to extract a grand total of £5 ($7.50) from the promoter for the première effort beneath the spotlights. But now, at least, Def Leppard could claim they were a genuine band. For all their painstaking deliberations in their ramshackle rehearsal room, the essence of any Hard Rock band was their live performance, and they were under no illusions about that. No matter how good they were behind closed doors they needed to prove themselves in front of an audience – and now they'd finally done it! And not only that, they'd also been paid for the privilege too.

So Def Leppard stopped being a fantasy in Joe's school exercise books and became a flesh-and-blood reality. And with that particular hurdle successfully jumped they could now look to the next great objective of any aspiring band: recording a demo!

CHAPTER THREE

THE KIDS ARE ALRIGHT

By the time Def Leppard felt themselves ready and able to enter a recording studio they had amassed themselves a sizeable repertoire of both cover and original numbers. Their own material displayed their more obvious influences at this early stage. One number entitled 'War Child' was a blatant Black Sabbath rip-off and soon found its way *out* of the set as Leppard became more and more melodically inclined. To this end 'Overture' harkened toward Canada's masters of Science Fiction/Fantasy Rock, Rush, while 'Answer To The Master' brought them more squarely back into the mainstream of rock with a sound not dissimilar to Judas Priest's. As far as audience favourites were concerned, though – and by this time Def Leppard were already building themselves an audience – the band had two rip-roaring classics up their well-muscled musical sleeves: 'Wasted', and what was to become something of an anthem for them, 'Getcha Rocks Off'.

In time both these tracks were to become, deservedly, acclaimed as Heavy Metal classics that were to herald the 'New Wave' of young songwriters as a force to be reckoned with. They were strident, energetic, and richly compelling numbers that belied Def Leppard's youth as composers. What they did display quite markedly was their obvious ear for both melody and a devastating 'catch-all' riff. These were numbers designed (and, indeed, *destined*) to have the punters 'headbanging' in the aisles – even if the actual thought of playing venues that possessed aisles seemed beyond the band at this time.

These, coupled with the cover numbers they still included, made up the Def Leppard set. Unlike American bands at this level who are expected to play a set derived exclusively from cover versions, British bands are required, almost by convention, to be much more adventurous when it comes to presenting original material. And as they set about the serious task of composing more of their own material the covers were slowly weeded out. Many of the these original compositions were later to find their way on to the Leppards' début album and it was obvious, even at this stage in their career, that they possessed a wealth of good material.

The problem they faced, then, before entering a studio to lay down a demo was in deciding which of many songs they should choose. And then there was the other small problem of finance.

It's one of those incongruous truths about rock 'n' roll – the original mode of teen rebellion against the restraints of the 'establishment' represented, in particular, by parents – that the fortunes of many would-be bands may rest solely and squarely in the hands of the parents whose rule they were *supposed* to be rebelling against. Fortuntely for Def Leppard the rule of Mr and Mrs Elliott over their son Joe was a benign one.

Mr Elliott Snr worked fitting radio and cassette players into cars. Both he and his wife doubtless viewed their son's activities, as most parents do, with a mild amusement coupled with a certain pride. The fact that Joe was doing something constructive to which he was obviously very dedicated – by this time most of Joe's non-working hours were spent with the band – must have pleased them and given no little cause for satisfaction, especially since it appeared to be doing so well. The newspapers in these days were filled with heady, almost hysterical reports of delinquent youths on orgies of 'glue sniffing' – one of the most disturbing trends highlighted by the outset of punk – or other equally unsavoury pastimes. What's worse, it was just such city kids as Joe, living in depressed areas like Sheffield, among whom such antisocial habits were most prevalent. That their son was engaged in a useful and absorbing activity – albeit a rock 'n' roll band – may well have come as something of a relief to Mr and Mrs Elliott and they were prepared to support him in this venture, at least until such time as he would settle down and do something 'proper'. It would be a long wait.

So when Def Leppard found themselves in a position of being ready, able, and willing to record a demo but severely lacking in finances, it was to Joe's parents that they turned for a hand-out. Although they themselves had scraped and scrounged as much money together as they could it clearly wasn't enough for what they needed; they required more and Mr and Mrs Elliott were co-opted as the patient benefactors.

Def Leppard's burgeoning career could have been brought crashing to a premature close at that moment had the Elliotts decided that enough was enough and that it really *was* time for their boy to do something sensible. But, thankfully, they just smiled and seemed content simply to let young Joe get on with whatever it was he needed the money for – they would never pretend to understand what he was up to – and loaned him the balance. Def Leppard, by that simple act of generosity, were saved from obscurity and Mr and Mrs Elliott set their son and his comrades off on a course set to reap rewards a multitude of times over from the sum they pressed into his hands.

The band then had to settle on which tracks to record. They needed to select songs that would display as many different facets to their style of music as possible. They wanted to show that they weren't simple riff-merchants – a criticism frequently laid at the feet of bands in the Hard Rock genre – but that they encompassed both power and subtlety in their music. At the same time they needed to prove that they were a commercially viable proposition to any prospective buyers who might chance to hear the finished demo. But, on the other side of the coin, they didn't want to betray their Hard Rock roots and end up with something crass and so abjectly commercial that it became teeny-bop mush.

In short they needed a marketable Hard Rock product, and in those days, when Heavy Metal was about as fashionable as yesterday's leftovers, that was going to prove no mean task. Since it simply wasn't record company policy at that stage to sign Hard Rock bands, for whom they believed there was no obvious commercial potential, the Leppards knew they had to come up with something more than a little special if it was going to attract any interest at all.

But then, since their avowed intention was to become renowned locally, scheming to impress the record companies in London probably wasn't in the forefront of their minds. They would go in and record their songs for a bit of a laugh without any serious consideration of whether they might actually get a recording contract out of it. But somewhere, lurking in the back of the mind of any youngster who goes into a recording studio to lay down a demo, is the dream that *this one* might make it, that *this one* might earn them that all important deal.

The tracks they eventually settled on were: 'Ride Into The Sun', 'Getcha Rocks Off', and 'Overture'. 'Ride Into The Sun', despite its science-fiction-style, almost Pink Floydesque, title was a basic girls/cars/boozin' & cruisin' song that jaunts along making perfect freeway music. Strange then that Sheffield has no freeways and no one in Def Leppard had even so much as laid eyes on one. But the slight American slant to the music was already present although that distinctly hard British edge to the guitar sound was still very much in evidence. This combination of traits was to become something of a Def Leppard trademark.

'Overture' was, in truth, a rather pretentious piece that borrowed heavily from the 'epic' sword & sorcery/fantasy exploits of Rush in their 'Caress of Steel'/'2112' days, with its acoustic opening and its tale of priests and the battles of oppressed peoples. If it is to be deemed 'pretentious' then this is really only the fault of Leppard's naïvety. Many, indeed *most*, new Hard Rock bands of this period fell into the trap of writing this type of material, attempting to ape their heroes and influences, the rock bands of the early '70s to whom these epic fantasies were basic fodder. These dinosaur bands were writing escapist songs for an escapist audience at a time when that kind of thing was very much in vogue. What most of these second-generation bands failed to appreciate was that all that had had its day and was simply no longer relevant or meaningful – not that it ever really had been. Fortunately Leppard managed to pull themselves away from the murky depths of that science fiction/fantasy rut in time and rarely looked back. But what still separated 'Overture' from the mish-mash of similar material penned by lesser bands and salvaged it from the ignominy of the junk heap – to which some more unkind critics might have felt inclined to consign it – was the sheer class of its musicianship. Here was a song being performed by musicians barely out of their adolescence but playing their instruments like true pro-fessionals many years their senior. The song dripped *class* and already Def Leppard were displaying not only their instrumental credentials but also a composing and arranging talent beyond their years. While the subject matter of 'Overture' may be well-worn and clichéd its actual execution is superb.

The demo's strongest number, which became the title track for the EP they cut from this exercise, was 'Getcha Rocks Off'. This track was the stand-out number and eventually became the song the EP was most remembered for. While early in their career Def Leppard may have enjoyed dabbling in songs con-cerning far-off galaxies, swords, and general sorcery, it was back solidly on Earth with both feet on the ground that they found their greatest strength. 'Getcha Rocks Off' is about as basic a rock 'n' roll lyric as you would ever care to find but this is where Def Leppard found home base with their audience. That, coupled with the fact that the song is played fast and furious over a devastating riff, ensured that it was to become a classic Heavy Metal anthem of its time. All the elements were there: it was played with energy and aggression, very much up-tempo, on a subject matter (sex) that anyone could relate to. It was simple, it was straightforward. In short, it was a winner.

So, in November 1978, Def Leppard – who then numbered Joe Elliott, Rick Savage, Pete Willis and Steve Clark, with Frank Noon on temporary hire on the drum stool – entered Fairview Studios to record their three selected tracks. Fairview Studios stands in a street with the unlikely – and rather *uninviting* – name of Great Cutter Lane in the city of Hull. Hull itself is situated on England's east coast, about fifty-five miles north-east of Sheffield. The studio is an eight-track and perfect for just the purpose to which Def Leppard were to put it: recording a demo.

CHAPTER FOUR

THE GREAT ROCK 'N' ROLL SWINDLE

The band emerged with what was in effect a master-tape that changed the course of their lives in a fashion they can only have dreamt about.

One of the first things Joe Elliott did with the cassette tapes run off the master was to package one off to Geoff Barton, then deputy editor of the now defunct weekly music paper *Sounds*. Barton received the tape along with a covering letter. The note came scribbled on paper headed with the logo *Def Leppard*, indicating that by now the band had begun to adopt a whole new professional attitude and approach to everything they were doing. Joe recognized the importance to a new band of some favourable press reaction and also knew whose goodwill had to be solicited in order to gain that good reaction.

It is often difficult for fans outside of the UK to appreciate the all-encompassing domination over style and product that the music press holds in Britain, particularly when viewed from the States where TV and radio vie for dominion and the press holds little sway. In Britain, however, the press enjoys the kind of authority that the broadcasters hold in America at a more grass-roots level. The press can make a band, especially if it latches on to them early in their career, and encouraging notices in the music papers can often bring bands that might otherwise languish in obscurity to the attention of the record companies. Similarly, rave reviews of bands can lead to deals being signed and fortunes, occasionally, being made. So as far as any new British band is concerned, press favour, though not necessarily *essential*, can make the path to stardom a whole lot less bumpy than it might otherwise appear. It is definitely something to be coveted.

On the other side of the coin the British music press is extremely fashion conscious. As already noted, fads and fashions in the British pop scene, unlike anywhere else in the world, follow Andy Warhol's famous dictum that everyone (or *thing*) deserves fifteen minutes of fame. Fashions come and go in the twinkling of an eye, each one following rapidly on the heels of its predecessor, and none of them lasting longer than a few brief, if brilliant, months. No other country on Earth has a media organ quite like the British music press. The press *reflects* this changing face of fashion rather than instigates it – the fact that the music press is, in general, weekly goes a long way to explaining this – and its journalists are eternally in search of 'the week's big thing' in their frantic attempts to be on top of the fluctuating situation, to have (or at least *appear* to have) their finger on the 'street-pulse'.

Since the predominant fashion in Britain in 1978 was punk – which in itself was unusual in that it lasted so long, years rather than just months – the music papers were overrun with it. And, in consequence, the most *un*fashionable thing you could possibly be into in 1978 was Heavy Metal, the total antithesis of punk and all that it stood for. In deference to this the column inches given to Heavy Metal by the music papers was, to say the least, extremely limited and no fashionable journalist would have been caught dead promoting a new Hard Rock band.

Sounds had picked up on the punk movement early and of the four leading British weeklies at the time (the other three being *NME*, *Melody Maker*, and *Record Mirror*) it became punk's foremost champion. Somewhere, in amongst all this, stood Geoff Barton, like a hang-over from a bygone era. Barton – known to his colleagues as 'Deaf' Barton because of his 'slight bias towards music of the Heavy Metal genre' and its effect on the hearing of its proponents – acted at the time like a small island of hope in a general sea of madness that flowed deep and forcibly at the time.

Barton was to become one of the key influential figures in the development of Def Leppard's career at this stage. He was already renowned for his over the top ravings on an assortment of Heavy Metal groups, most notably Kiss, whose cause he championed in this country and for whom he gained much needed exposure. For while *Sounds* had pretty much become *the* punk paper, it was also the only paper that gave any serious coverage to the Heavy Rock acts. And this in itself was in no small way due to the contribution of Barton.

So when Joe looked around for someone to whom Def Leppard could plead their cause, he turned to *Sounds* and to Geoff Barton in particular since, at the time, he was quite probably *the* voice of Heavy Metal. This turned out to be a very opportune move on Joe's part and Barton was soon foaming at the mouth over the three-track cassette and itching to get out and see the band live.

That opportunity, however, would not arise until the following year due, mainly, to the pressures and limited time for actual reporting in his job as deputy editor. Def Leppard's potential saviour found himself too tied to his desk in London to help these five lads in Sheffield get off the ground . . . at least for the time being.

Meanwhile, for Def Leppard, after the new and alien environment of the recording studio, it was back to the stage and back to gigging, playing such improbable venues as Dale Miners' Welfare Club and High Green Liberal Club. If there was a gig to be played, they'd play it.

And at one such gig they found themselves supporting another local Sheffield band, The Human League. A more unlikely coupling of acts is, perhaps, difficult to conceive. The Human League later fell under the gaze of David Bowie, went through some personnel changes, and emerged as one of the forerunners of the 'synth-pop' explosion of the early '80s.

Curiously enough though, the bands came to represent the opposite ends of the spectrum of a movement that the Americans would come to label as 'The British Invasion'. The Human League had released their smash-hit album *Dare* while Def Leppard were beginning to break through with their second album, *High 'n' Dry*.

However, they were still no closer, musically, than they had been on that night in Sheffield when they appeared on the same bill. While The Human League dabbled in the fashionable synthesizer-drenched end of the pop market Def Leppard were unleashing the full fury of their Heavy Rock arsenal. How these two bands – about as chalk-and-cheese as it was then possible to get – came to be playing together is unclear but there was someone present from a local paper to record the event for posterity. And this reporter could not be described as a Def Leppard fan, and yet, strangely enough, he was to make his quite unintentional mark on their career.

In his review of the Leppards the reporter referred to their style of music as 'bludgeon riffola'. The phrase was meant as a put-down of the band and everything about them. But then Leppard knew they weren't a fashionably 'hip' item and also knew they could expect little better from the press. And, quite frankly, they didn't care one way or the other what the press – at least at the level this particular journalist was writing – thought of them or their music. But what was undeniable was just how close to the mark the reporter had come with that phrase to summing Def Leppard up. 'Bludgeon riffola' was evidently poison to the writer, but to the band and their fans it was meat. And it also had a nice ring to it: Bludgeon Riffola! What was meant as a slagging would be turned right around and used for the band's own ends. Def Leppard took the phrase that was intended to damn them and went right ahead and named their own record label with it! Bludgeon Riffola Records was born.

On the surface Def Leppard started life as the antithesis of everything that punk rock stood for. At a time when *not* being able to play an instrument was almost considered a virtue, Def Leppard were masters of theirs; while the punks tried to dress down and look as tatty as possible, Def Leppard dressed *up*; while the punks sang about boredom and anarchy, Def Leppard sang about girls and cars; while the punks tried to outrage, Def Leppard tried to entertain.

But punk rock undoubtedly changed the face of modern music and affected the music industry itself like nothing since the arrival of the Beatles. And, if nothing else, it made one vastly important – and, for once, *constructive* – contribution to the industry and one that Def Leppard were to employ to their own (considerable) advantage. Punk re-invented and re-instated the independent record label.

Punk didn't originate the independent label – they'd been around, after all, since the earliest days of the imported American blues, decades before – but what it did do was popularize the idea and open the way for a lot of bands to get their product on to vinyl and into shops, including Def Leppard. It has to be remembered that these were the days when records came in two forms: vinyl and cassette. Inventions like CD, CD-i, and DAT were still on the drawing boards. And the attraction of vinyl was that it was cheap and it still looked professional.

The punks were suspicious – and to a degree not without good cause – of the major record companies, and many punk bands preferred to sign to smaller, independent labels. But beyond that they even showed that it was possible to apply the concept of DIY to the record business. The punk movement proved that it was an entirely practical proposition, even if you couldn't get a deal with a small label, to establish your own and put the record out yourself. Literally hundreds of labels came into being, often with only one act on the roster, the band who'd set it up.

The process was simple. You recorded a demo, had it pressed up on to vinyl, and released it, all by yourself, without a major record company coming anywhere near. And that suited the punks, with their philosophy of 'big is bad, small is beautiful', perfectly. Depending on the number of copies you could afford to have pressed you might then get the thing distributed nationwide by one of several independent distribution companies that were set up to cope with the wealth of new material that required shipping. But usually it was done on a mail-order basis – operated, more often than not, out of someone's front room – or by the band taking batches of their newly pressed single personally to friendly record shops in their area, who would then display it. This kind of operation opened the way for many bands and also their labels. Some more famous examples that emerged from the punk rock label proliferation were Rough Trade, Factory, and Two-Tone, who each sponsored many up-and-coming talented acts. Bludgeon Riffola Records, in a way, had much the same effect on the one and only act on its roster, Def Leppard. The label may never have spread further than the band's own product but its importance in the Leppard history is none the less crucial.

How the reporter took to having his words thrown back at him in this manner is not known, but it is likely not kindly, especially as it turned out to be such a roaring success, contrary to his estimation. Before the band later resurrected the label, Bludgeon Riffola Records had a brief lifespan, but it shone brilliantly for all that. There was only ever one record issued on the label in this first incarnation, at the beginning of 1979, but that proved to be a very significant release: the *Getcha Rocks Off* EP of which the original pressing ran to only 1,000 copies.

The *Getcha Rocks Off* EP has since become not only an acknowledged classic of its time but also a much sought after item among record collectors. The original red-label pressing can fetch, at the time of writing, anything up to £250 ($375), and the yellow-labelled re-issue a more modest £15 ($22). But at the time Def Leppard were hardly overwhelmed and coped with what demand there was on a purely personal mail-order service manned by Joe's girlfriend. They also dropped off a batch to a local record shop called Revolution Records, managed by a man called Peter Martin, where Joe was a regular customer.

Peter Martin was in contact with a record plugger for Arista Records called Frank Stuart-Brown – the pair of them had both worked for WEA Records some years before as sales representatives – and got him to listen to the EP which had begun to pick up some notice after Geoff Barton had featured it in his *Sounds* 'playlist', where the journalists would name their favourite records of the week. Frank Stuart-Brown had no hesitation: 'I'd never been so sure of anything in my life, this band were going to be huge!' Within forty-eight hours the two were in partnership again, this time with a pitch for management.

The pair of them set to work immediately and quickly met up with the Leppards who, by this time, had recruited a fifteen-year-old schoolboy drummer by the name of Rick Allen. He it was who brought to an end the stream of temporary skin-beaters who'd passed through the ranks of the band: with his succession to the stool he made the spot his own. So, quite suddenly, Def Leppard not only had a new, and permanent, drummer, they also had a management team on board. Frank Stuart-Brown and Peter Martin took over their affairs there and then. What impressed them as much as the obvious quality of their musicianship was the band's extremely positive attitude toward playing. At a period when attitudes were uniformly negative – another one of the legacies of the punk movement, the overriding sense of *nihilism* they brought to bear on everything they touched; like a kind of King Midas in reverse! – they came like a breath of fresh air.

Frank Stuart-Brown had worked for some time in the music business and was well connected, both to record companies and the media. At the time he believed he would be able to negotiate a deal for Def Leppard within eighteen months such was the quality of their work and his absolute conviction that he'd struck gold! In fact it took Messrs Martin and Stuart-Brown just eight months after their initial meeting with the band to score them a major deal. But their initial efforts were far from fruitful.

In February 1979 Def Leppard's new managers travelled to London to extol the virtues of their band to all the major record companies – and not one of them was interested! The reason for the cold-shoulder treatment was quite obvious: they were trying to hawk a new Heavy Metal act and Heavy Metal, as everybody knew, was definitely *out*! Punk had decimated a once thriving Heavy Rock scene and most of the supergroups who had been born out of that genre in the early '70s were now just distant memories, scorned and despised, the floor having been whipped from under their feet. The record companies were extremely cautious when it came to Heavy Metal bands. All the media told them that Heavy Metal was dead, and indeed the two recognizably Heavy Metal bands who *did* have deals were struggling. Motorhead – who in actual fact were closer to being a punk band anyway, starting life touring as part of a punk package that included The Damned and The Adverts, hardly hard-core Heavy Metal! – had already parted company with United Artists (now part of the EMI group) and their début on the small independent label, Chiswick, sold respectably but not enough to send shivers of concern down the spines of A&R chiefs around the other companies. The other new Heavy Metal band, Saxon – the first of the 'New Wave of British Heavy Metal' groups to sign a deal – had released their own début on the Carrere label (now defunct), another independent, but that again hardly caused a murmur and soon sank without trace. Both bands were to break the big time by the following year, Motorhead having released their classic *Overkill* album, and Saxon having scored some notable success with their hit single, 'Strangers in the Night', and the accompanying album *Wheels of Steel*. But in 1979 they were still struggling to keep their heads above water and this had not gone unnoticed amongst the major labels. Perhaps understandably, in the light of all this, no one felt particularly inclined to chance their arm on yet *another* untried and untested Heavy Metal band. So, for the moment at least, they all passed Def Leppard by.

But Frank Stuart-Brown was undeterred and was already

bringing his contacts in the radio world to bear. First, there were the local radio stations; and then there was national BBC Radio One.

Radio operates quite differently in Britain from the way it does in the States, for instance, where there are innumerable stations, some specializing exclusively in rock music. But with Radio One, and beneath that the network of local radio stations run either by the BBC or the commercial broadcasting company, the IBA, the set-up is still basically pop fodder. Although, that said, these stations do cater more readily for various local needs or requests.

Most DJs on Radio One – at the time the only nationally broadcast pop station – had served their apprenticeships by working on these local stations. They used to come up through the pirate radio network but that breeding ground dried up when the government started cracking down in the late '60s and early '70s.

One such DJ was Andy Peebles, whom Stuart-Brown knew when he worked on Piccadilly Radio in Manchester in England's north-east. Peebles had now moved on to Radio One and had his own show in the evenings. As a favour to Stuart-Brown, Peebles aired the *Getcha Rocks Off* EP over the national airwaves and the snowball started rolling. Despite its apparent lack of appeal – being obviously and unashamedly Heavy Metal – Peebles stuck with it and played it every night for several weeks. Another DJ, John Peel – who was considered something of a guru or godfather to the punk movement and was renowned (or perhaps 'infamous' would be a better description) for his championing of obscure punk bands, particularly foreign ones – even managed to give the EP some airtime, although it has to be said rather more reluctantly. And Tommy Vance, for many years the DJ in charge of the *only* nationally broadcast rock programme, played it enthusiastically too, after Peebles had brought it to everyone's attention.

This was a carefully orchestrated attack on two fronts. Stuart-Brown had not only convinced the national radio DJs to plug Def Leppard but also the grass-roots level local radio programmes. All around the country Stuart-Brown had twisted arms and cajoled DJs into playing *Getcha Rocks Off*, so it was quite possible for any kid in the country to tune to his local radio rock programme and hear this unknown band called Def Leppard and *then* turn his dial to find the *same* band being broadcast over the national airwaves!

Within the short space of a couple of months Frank Stuart-Brown had set about persuading the country that there was a huge rock band in existence warranting all this airplay when in fact the biggest gig Def Leppard had performed in their career was to five hundred people at Sheffield Polytechnic! And on the live front, as far as their manager was concerned: 'They were just five inexperienced kids . . . but there was something there that was exciting.' Stuart-Brown's manipulation of Def Leppard's image was quite masterful and it was beginning to pay off.

Back in Sheffield, Joe and Rick Savage were doing some record plugging – or, more specifically, *Getcha Rocks Off* plugging – of their own. The local commercial station in Sheffield is called Radio Hallam and both Leppards were avid listeners because one DJ in particular, Colin Slade, tended to play their kind of music. Slade had his own Heavy Rock show on Monday nights.

Joe and Sav had been regular listeners to Slade's programme for some time and were always entering the competitions he would run. At the beginning of their career they had consulted the people at Hallam, seeking general advice about how to get themselves off the ground. So Colin Slade knew both the names of Elliott and Savage *and* the group Def Leppard, but had never actually made the connection between them. Then one day Joe and Sav went to the radio station to collect their prizes for a competition they had entered and this time won. They introduced themselves to Slade and then mentioned that they were in fact Def Leppard as well, at least 40 per cent of it. Then they asked the sympathetic DJ to organize a studio session for them for broadcast. Colin Slade immediately took an interest in the band, seeing them play live several times thereafter. He offered them constructive criticism on their songs and recalls in particular one piece of advice he gave to Joe: 'I remember commenting to Joe that he'd have to learn to sing properly! He sings from his throat and was always knackering his throat up. And he did in fact, I believe, have to go and get some formal instruction to learn how to sing properly around the time of the first album. He had to learn the hard way!'

So when the *Getcha Rocks Off* EP was pressed they sent one over to Colin Slade and he promptly put the thing on the air. The morning after the EP was first broadcast on Radio Hallam (its début broadcast anywhere in the world) Peter Martin's Revolution Records found itself inundated with demands for the disc. By the end of the morning the batch had completely sold out. The snowball started gathering momentum.

Through the efforts of Colin Slade and Radio Hallam Def Leppard's local following boomed! Soon after, with plugs from Andy Peebles, rave reviews in *Sounds*, and local radio stations nationwide picking up on it, the initial pressing had completely sold out through mail-order and was quickly re-issued. The only difference between the original (and consequently far more valuable) pressing and the second pressing was the colour of the label. As already mentioned, the original was coloured red while the re-issue was yellow. It came packaged in a white sleeve with a picture of a leopard listening intently to an old gramophone – an obvious and not too subtle lampoon of the famous 'Nipper' pose that the original HMV (His Master's Voice) label had always employed as their logo. It also harked back to the days of Deaf Leopard and the drawings Joe came up with in his art classes. On the back was a small photo of each member of the band including the now departed Frank Noon.

The demand for this product was staggeringly high and it eventually clocked up sales figures of something in the region of 24,000 copies. For a project that, according to Frank Stuart-Brown, was originally 'done for a laugh' this was a quite extraordinary achievement. It featured prominently in the Heavy

Metal charts for some months and even reached Number 84 in the national pop charts. At last the industry began to wake up to the fact that Heavy Metal was far from dead. And if Frank Stuart-Brown was to be believed, it was alive and kicking and living in Sheffield under the name of Def Leppard. The buzz was on.

Frank Stuart-Brown had, through sheer dogged hard work on the part of himself and his partner, Peter Martin, succeeded in conning the country into believing Def Leppard were something they (as yet anyway) quite clearly weren't: a huge band.

The hype had taken off and by some judicious plugging in all the right places, that hype was bought, lock, stock, and barrel. In essence the band that was being sold didn't really exist, at least not at quite the same magnitude as their managers had portrayed them. But that didn't really matter. What did matter was the same band that every major record company in London had turned down flat as being part of a dead and buried movement were now receiving mega-plugging on Radio One and local radio stations all over the country. What Stuart-Brown and Martin had offered them on a plate at the beginning of the year, come the summer they were preparing themselves to hold back until just the right moment. The final icing on this hyped-up cake was about to come, in print and on air.

Geoff Barton, the *Sounds* journalist who was one of the first to receive a demo tape of the EP at the end of the previous year, had now managed to free himself from the manacles of his sub-editing desk long enough finally to make the trip to Sheffield. By this time the EP had taken off in a big way and Barton's enthusiasm was running rampant, and he was indeed in some way responsible for the success of *Getcha Rocks Off*. Accompanied by photographer Ross Halfin they journeyed northwards in search of this new megaband.

What they found was something closer to the truth: Def Leppard playing Crookes Workingmen's Club to a disappointingly thin on the ground audience, although this was largely due to the gig clashing with Status Quo's appearance that same night at the Sheffield City Hall. The band, far from being the megastars the journalists might have been led to believe, were in fact five ordinary working-class kids who happened to have an extraordinary gift for Heavy Rock music.

But Barton's enthusiasm remained undimmed and when his article appeared in *Sounds* a few weeks later in June – incidentally, the first major coverage Def Leppard had ever received – it was spread across three pages under the title of the 'New Wave Of British Heavy Metal'. A slogan had been coined. It was an event all but unheard of in the trendy days of the punk-saturated music press – three entire pages devoted to a Heavy Metal band! Totally unbelievable!

And the band could hardly credit their luck either, especially when the same week as Geoff Barton's feature was published Def Leppard had their first session broadcast on Radio One. The timing was perfect!

Shortly before, in May, Colin Slade delivered on his promise to get them a Radio Hallam session broadcast, too. They recorded six tracks: 'Glad I'm Alive', 'When The Walls Come Tumblin' Down', 'Sorrow Is A Woman', 'Answer To The Master', and 'Beyond The Temple', three of which later appeared on their first album, proving that by now their repertoire of original material had become quite extensive.

But it was the combination of their Radio One session broadcast and their unprecedented spread in *Sounds* that really clinched it for them and sealed the knot of their fate. As Frank Stuart-Brown put it: 'It was a question of "Take Your Pick!" We weren't being greedy but we were after the best long-term deal.'

What had happened was that all the top A&R men in the country – the very people who had turned their noses up at Def Leppard only a few months before – were hammering on the managers' door waving contracts. Stuart-Brown's media manipulation had been so cleverly orchestrated all he had to do now was pick the company offering the best deal. The hype had worked even faster and more lucratively than ever they had anticipated.

Shortly after the Radio One session Stuart-Brown organized a showcase gig for the band at the Retford Porterhouse in Nottinghamshire, in the English Midlands, with the A&R executives clamouring to get in. In the end it was Rodger Bain, head of A&R at Phonogram Records (part of the worldwide Polygram group) who was not only the first to offer a deal but who also offered the best long-term proposition. On the table was a deal that promised total advances of £120,000 ($180,000) and ten points (i.e. 10% of the retail sales on records). For an unheard of – or at least comparatively 'unheard of' – act that no one had really seen, this was an extremely lucrative deal for the band and also showed just how anxious the record company were to grab hold of this exciting new talent that had already, off their own backs, created such a nationwide stir. In the event it proved to be one of the soundest and most profitable investments the company had ever made, but not before a few heart-beats had been missed along the way!

In August of that year, 1979, they played their most prestigious gig to date when they appeared on the bill at an outdoor show sponsored by Radio Hallam in a park in front of the largest crowd they had yet encountered – several thousand people. They were going to need every particle of experience they could muster over the next few months, and this show would prove invaluable. It consolidated their home support and gave them a much needed taste of what would be required of them in years to come: the ability and confidence to entertain thousands of fans at one time.

With that show behind them they would bid a fond farewell to Sheffield for the time being. They already had a recording contract signed, sealed, and delivered and now Phonogram found themselves with the problem of having a priority act on their books that virtually nobody knew about. Nobody, that is, apart from those who had tuned in to the various radio broadcasts. And, worse still, even they knew nothing about what the band actually looked like! Obviously one of the first things that needed to be done with Def Leppard was to get them out in front of the public who had so eagerly snapped up *Getcha Rocks Off*. What they needed now was to go out on tour.

The usual method for breaking a band like Def Leppard – the tried and trusted method – would be to have them record a single and then send them out on a tour of the clubs. On the one hand this would promote the single, on the other it would get them better known. But Def Leppard were different. Firstly, they already had a hit single of sorts with the EP; and secondly, the fans had been led to expect something like the second coming of Led Zeppelin! To be seen traipsing round the club circuit after the build-up Frank Stuart-Brown had engineered for them would have been seen as a real step backwards. Of course, with Leppard's almost total inexperience of gigging outside the Sheffield area, this probably would have still, despite the possible short-term repercussions, been the smartest move to make. With hindsight, they could have built themselves up a loyal following on a cross-country basis similar to the support they had gathered in their home town. But at the time things looked very different. Def Leppard, Phonogram decided, needed a high profile and for a high profile they needed a big tour.

The tour they landed up on was headlined by American singer/guitarist Sammy Hagar who later went on to replace David Lee Roth in Van Halen. Leppard got the tour on the suggestion of Martin Cox who was then label manager at Capitol Records, Hagar's record company. It was on his recommendation that the promoter, John Curd, placed the untried band in the support slot.

Hagar was considered part of Geoff Barton's much vaunted New Wave Of Heavy Metal (this time 'American Division') alongside Van Halen and Ted Nugent. In truth, though, Sammy Hagar had been around since the early '70s when he fronted one of America's most influential Heavy Metal outfits, Montrose. Ted Nugent had been around even longer, since the mid-'60s, with his band The Amboy Dukes, so really only Van Halen were truly new. Nevertheless, both Hagar and Nugent were attempting to break the British market, this always being considered the prize jewel in any Heavy Rock band's eyes since Britain was always considered the home of Heavy Metal. With such a resurgence of interest, then, in Heavy Rock Hagar obviously deemed it an auspicious moment to make his entry.

However, Sammy Hagar was still pretty much an unknown quantity in the UK. Montrose remained a relatively 'cult' band in British circles. He needed a band who could sell tickets for him on his brief four-date tour. And Def Leppard were fairly confident they could sell the tickets; they just needed a tour. So a deal was struck for both acts' mutual convenience. Strictly speaking it was a double-headliner tour rather than a tour with 'Sammy Hagar as headline act and Def Leppard as support', but in the end it made no odds. The important thing, as far as Def Leppard were concerned, was that they were out treading the boards on a proper tour for the first time in their career! And for the first time, the punters, apart from the select few who had seen the band in and around Sheffield, could at last find out just who it was they'd been listening to all this time.

What must have struck many fans as the most surprising thing about Def Leppard was just how incredibly young they looked; hardly any older, in fact, than most of the kids in the audience. None the less, the reaction was encouraging, based partly *in spite of* their youth – there was no disputing the maturity of their performance and delivery of their material – and partly *because of* their youth. Whereas most of these kids' heroes amongst the 'Old Wave' of rock bands played on massive stages, becoming untouchable, unreachable figures, with Def Leppard you could really imagine it was you up there. To many of the punters who saw them on that tour they must have appeared like older brothers on stage; it wasn't so hard to pretend it could really be you instead.

The other great capital Def Leppard had always possessed as

a band was the simple fact that they also looked good. But on the other hand, they still managed to look ordinary. This was no mean feat. They had never been content to walk in off the streets in jeans and T-shirts to go straight up on stage and start playing like most of their contemporaries did, both in the punk bands and the 'NWOBHM' acts. Def Leppard made a conscious effort to look the part when they were in front of an audience. For a long time Joe sported a slick pair of PVC 'leather look' jeans – his meagre financial resources wouldn't stretch to a real pair – and silk shirts, while the two guitarists and Sav dressed similarly 'up', most notably Steve Clark with a pair of skin-tight leopard-skin jeans. Later, after a few pay cheques had arrived, they donned an assortment of silk kimonos and spandex slacks, such was the call of Heavy Metal fashion at the time. But whatever they wore, they at least looked like a professional band who meant business, while still managing to look like the fans' older brothers; so they were, for a time at least, getting the best of both worlds.

When Def Leppard initially signed to Phonogram the first thing the company did was re-issue the EP under their own rock label, Vertigo – already home to such luminaries as Black Sabbath, Status Quo, Dire Straits, and the band's heroes, Thin Lizzy – but the first original release was issued to coincide with the Sammy Hagar tour. The track chosen for the A-side – and remember, in those days singles had such things as A-sides! – was the stage favourite 'Wasted', a storming pile-driver of a rocker – at least on stage it was. On the flip side was a new song, 'Hello America', which showed the more melodic facet to their character.

On paper it certainly seemed a sensible enough choice, displaying two diverse sides to the band's repertoire, but, as is often the case, reality didn't match up to the expectation the idea first engendered. The basic problem was one of presentation, although the actual *sound* of the record in the ears of some left something to be desired, too. It was also the beginning of a rut that Def Leppard found themselves pushed into, quite beyond their control or, for that matter, understanding; a downhill slide that was to climax the following year at the Reading Festival and would take a further three years for the band finally to halt.

It was a small, niggling complaint really and one the band didn't feel in a strong enough position within the record company to push to get changed. Basically, having so recently been signed they didn't want to start creating waves and getting themselves a reputation as one of those 'difficult' bands to work with.

The 'Wasted' single came in a picture sleeve and on the back was a picture of a white, silver, and gold stiletto-ed boot. The same boot, reduced to black and white, was emblazoned all over the advertisements the record company took out, too. Clearly, someone in design had decided this boot was to be the Def Leppard logo but, as far as Def Leppard were concerned, it *definitely* wasn't what they were all about! There seemed to be a communication problem.

Joe later complained that it was the management's idea and that the idea was, presumably, to present an image of Def Leppard as a slick, sophisticated, high-class band. But it didn't work out that way. As Heavy Metal had always been a traditionally working-class, rough, tough street-wise sort of music, the use of the boot image merely served to label the band as something approaching Glam Rock. Glam Rock was, in many ways, not wildly dissimilar but, in these instances, the devil is in the detail and this detail was to dog the band, insignificant as it might appear on the surface.

By coincidence the same tag 'Glam Rock' – the labelling device that both record companies and press alike are so fond of in Britain – was later to cause Phil Collen's band Girl such aggravation and open hostility. This kind of reaction was the last thing Def Leppard wanted or needed. *They* were more concerned with the production of the tracks, particularly 'Wasted'. The song to some listeners seemed devoid of the raunch and aggressive power it had on stage. The producer,

Nick Tauber, went on to do a fine job on the début Marillion album, *Script For A Jester's Tears*, but Marillion, a progressive rock band, were very much in tune with Tauber's production *forte*. Def Leppard clearly were not so well matched with him from their point of view.

But whatever protests the band *did* raise were unheeded while they simply assumed that the record company probably knew best – and quietly let the matter drop perhaps unlike more experienced acts. So their début Phonogram single emerged as scheduled and trouble began.

But this trouble would take a while to manifest itself and meantime Def Leppard were still riding a high from the success of the EP, their signing, and their first proper tour, which culminated in a show at London's prestigious Hammersmith Odeon, since renamed the Apollo. The Hammersmith Odeon was a three-and-a-half thousand seat hall which was actually built as a cinema though it is rarely used for that purpose nowadays. It was one of those venues by which a band could measure their success and progress; it was a pinnacle that had to be scaled and conquered. To play the Hammersmith Odeon was an ambition that all young bands would aspire to and one they would usually achieve only after years of hard work and arduous touring of the club circuit building up enough of a following to reach that vaunted position.

For Def Leppard, however, all of whom with the exception of Joe were still in their teens at the time, the first gig they *ever* *played* in London was the Hammersmith Odeon! They had simply by-passed the tried-and-trusted method of touring that club circuit before eventually graduating to play the Odeon. Def Leppard went straight in at the top – or if not the top, at least very close to the summit – not to mention the deep end. But they passed the test, and with honours, and now they could move on to the next hurdle.

If the object up at the Phonogram marketing division was to keep Def Leppard in the public eye then they certainly went the right way about it. The band barely had time to collect their thoughts and catch their breath before they were packaged off again, this time as support on the AC/DC tour. Now this was *very big news*!

AC/DC had released *Highway To Hell* in 1979 and it was their biggest seller to date. It had entered the American charts and things were beginning to open up for them like never before, although the band had been immensely popular in Britain almost from the word go, due partially to the larger-than-life personalities and on-stage antics of guitarist Angus Young and then vocalist Bon Scott, as well as their no-holds-barred powerhouse Heavy Metal sound. Sadly, though, it was also to be Bon Scott's final tour. He died the following February following a spate of heavy drinking. This was another aspect of life in the fast lane that would later come back to haunt the Leppards themselves. But meanwhile, this final tour for Bon Scott was, at least, a roaring success.

Def Leppard calculate that they played to something in excess of 40,000 people over the course of those two tours, which must certainly have tied in with what the record company considered to be giving the band a high profile! A high profile, however, was the last thing Frank Stuart-Brown wanted for the band at this stage.

His strategy, up till that point, had worked perfectly. He had, in effect, persuaded the record company into signing the band to a major deal under the impression that they were an already established act. He had been using the contacts he'd made in the media working for record companies like WEA, Atlantic, Private Stock, and latterly Arista as well as with such acts at the Bay City Rollers, Gary Glitter, Showaddywaddy, and David Soul, and could therefore claim that he knew 'how to build an act'. He managed to manipulate these contacts into creating the myth of a megaband called Def Leppard. Stuart-Brown himself had believed from the moment he heard the EP that Leppard *could* be as big as he was claiming they already were, but he also knew the perils of the kind of game he had been playing with the record company. They, too, believed they had a big band on their books, ready and able to play big venues. The truth of the matter was they simply weren't that big, or that ready, or that able, at least not yet. Having built up this image of a big, established band in order to sell the hype – which was duly bought – Stuart-Brown then needed to with-draw the band rapidly from the public gaze, having given them a brief glimpse of his emerging super-group over the four dates of the Sammy Hagar tour.

According to Stuart-Brown, Def Leppard needed the AC/DC tour 'like a hole in the head'. The result threw a spanner into the working of his Master Plan, and that result was 'over-exposure'. A rift began to develop between the band and their management.

Frank Stuart-Brown's plan was to allow them to play the occasional show around the country – unpublicized except for purely local promotion – in order to gain the gigging experience which they were woefully lacking. He could see the gaping flaw in his hype of Def Leppard and it was quite simply that anyone, particularly in the music business, who went to see this suppos-edly big band would see instead only a bunch of teenagers on stage at the very start of their career. The scheme to avert this danger was to have them play as many low-key gigs as possible avoiding all press and music industry people in general and, indeed, any more punters than were absolutely necessary. And the scheme, for a time anyway, worked perfectly.

By the time they signed the deal and took off on the Sammy Hagar tour the buzz was on and the band themselves were gigged enough to carry this leap into the big league without too much trouble. Four gigs throughout the country were just enough to whet the appetites of the fans who had waited so long to see the band after they'd taken so forcefully to the EP. With these appetites dutifully stimulated the plan then said they should be whipped away into seclusion leaving the punters hungry for more. The idea was that come the New Year when Def Leppard embarked on a club tour of their own the story would have spread by word of mouth as to just what a hot property this band actually were. Result: sell-out club tour for which the band would have been thoroughly prepared and could take in their stride. They would then have begun building a solid hard-core following throughout the country by playing these smaller venues that could then translate into record sales. At least that was the plan.

And that plan, as it stood, seemed fool-proof, but maybe it hadn't been fully explained to or fully understood by the band themselves. They too, to a degree, had been caught up in the hype and couldn't understand why they were getting a major record deal, a major tour, and yet were expected to play small, low-key gigs that no one was going to come to! And then when they were offered the AC/DC tour straight after a very successful stint with Sammy Hagar maybe they couldn't understand why their management didn't want them to do it.

It seems that the band and their management were at cross purposes because a rift had developed between them. So by the end of the AC/DC tour, with 40,000 eager punters all having had their curiousity about this band Def Leppard satisfied, it seemed, at least to Frank Stuart-Brown, that everyone who had wanted to see the band had now done so and that his plan was beginning to fall to pieces. But, of course, by that time Frank Stuart-Brown and his partner Peter Martin were no longer managers of Def Leppard!

AC/DC were one of the bands on the roster of the Leber–Krebs management team based out of New York. Steve Leber and David Krebs formed one of the most powerful management partnerships of recent years, guiding the careers of such notable acts as Aerosmith and Ted Nugent. On their team was a New Yorker in his late twenties called Peter Mensch. Mensch was a hot-shot tour manager who had successfully handled the affairs of both The Scorpions, the biggest German rock band ever, and now AC/DC, who held the same status in Australia. He brought AC/DC to Britain that autumn and immediately encountered the support act, Def Leppard. Very shortly after, Def Leppard had a new manager.

Peter Mensch, according to a now understandably somewhat bitter Frank Stuart-Brown, 'thought he'd come in with a big band – he had been duped just as much as the media had'. But it was clear that Mensch cut an extremely impressive figure and Def Leppard seem to have taken little time in moving away from their present management team.

'Def Leppard thought he [Peter Mensch] was the bee's knees,' explains Stuart-Brown on why he and his partner were suddenly ditched by the band. 'This was American management, this was the big time!'

Def Leppard were obviously over-awed by the fast-talking whiz-kid whose impressive record spoke volumes for what he could do for the band, and, indeed, did eventually deliver. But Frank Stuart-Brown's claim that Peter Mensch had swallowed his hyping of Def Leppard also holds water. Had Mensch known the backlash that was quietly gathering momentum around the next corner, lying in wait for Def Leppard, he might have thought twice about his new band.

At this time everything in the Def Leppard garden looked exceptionally rosy. The AC/DC tour went off well and Def Leppard scored some success in the *Melody Maker* readers' poll published shortly after the end of the tour in November. They were voted in fourth place in the 'Brightest Hope' category. Even more surprisingly they were placed sixth in the same category in the *NME* poll. The *NME* is easily the most radical and politically active of Britain's music press and has never been known for its support of Heavy Rock bands. To score at all in such a poll, let alone so highly above far more 'street-credible' acts like The Pretenders or Secret Affair, can be viewed as something of a minor miracle. If nothing else these poll results showed that Def Leppard had impressed a good many people on their outings with Sammy Hagar and AC/DC.

From this point onwards everything seemed to turn *downwards* for Def Leppard, at least as far as Britain was concerned; it took them three full years to begin to re-establish themselves as a major force in their native land. Quite where the blame lies for the downturn in Leppard's affairs in Britain will never really become clear and the most likely answer is that a portion of the culpability lies in each of four corners: with the band themselves for attempting to jump the gun, believing themselves to be as big as the media had made them out to be; with the record company for pushing the band too hard and too fast in what they believed to be the right direction; with Frank Stuart-Brown and Peter Martin for creating a hype around Def Leppard so dense that even the band themselves sometimes apparently had trouble distinguishing between it and the reality of the situation; and with Pete Mensch for taking on what was then a young, inexperienced, and impressionable band.

Of course it's impossible to say now whether Frank Stuart-Brown and Peter Martin could have averted the backlash that seems inevitably to follow any hype, but certainly they had kept everything fairly well under control up till that point and seemed to know how to develop their act from a standing start onwards. But then could they have achieved the extraordinary level of success that Def Leppard now enjoy around the world, and particularly in the States, under the astute guidance of Peter Mensch and his Stateside partner Cliff Burnstein?

However, what can be stated as fact is that Def Leppard under their new Leber–Krebs management deal, promptly parted company with Heavy Publicity, the PR company Stuart-Brown and Martin had wooed to work on behalf of the band. Heavy Publicity, now defunct, at the time handled the press for practically every major Heavy Rock act in the country, both home-grown and visiting from abroad. But they wanted no part of any more Leber–Krebs acts due to the financial wrangles they were engaged in. This certainly didn't help Leppard's cause when the full fury of the press backlash began to strike at the beginning of the new year.

Secondly, there followed a long legal dispute between the band and their former management which was eventually settled only by Stuart-Brown and Martin being awarded royalties from the sales of the first two albums – which, after the success of the third album and subsequent re-issues, proved rather lucrative.

Thirdly, in addition to all the trouble over management, Def Leppard's position took a real battering in the next few months despite all the hard work that both the band and their managers had lavished on their careers up to that point.

The hype had been sold and the manipulation that brought it off was nothing short of masterful. In the end, though, Def Leppard were caught up by their own naïvety and their dreams of rock 'n' roll stardom. To a large degree they *were* still just kids on stage imitating their heroes, but what kept them afloat, sustaining them until the light eventually showed itself at the end of their own peculiar tunnel, was the fact that they really were very talented musicians who also believed in themselves enough to hold on to their dreams. The year following their breakthrough, starting with the Sammy Hagar and AC/DC tours, was to prove an extremely exacting one on them emotionally when it appeared that everybody had turned against them. In a way they'd really had it too easy and had never 'paid their dues' as is the rock 'n' roll tradition for all bands who ever aspire to greatness. But particularly over the next twelve months Def Leppard were to pay those dues several times over, ultimately proving both their worth and the fact that they really *did* deserve the extraordinary success that was to come their way.

Frank Stuart-Brown and Peter Martin had given up practically everything to devote themselves to Def Leppard's early rise. Were they the first real casualties of the band's rise to success? If they were, they certainly weren't to be the last.

Peter Mensch eventually worked his way out of the Leber–Krebs management empire to set up his own with Def Leppard as his prize jewel. But he still had to wait considerably longer than he doubtless first anticipated before they finally turned up trumps for him.

Def Leppard, meanwhile, were having to turn their thoughts

to the next major obstacle. They were now being expected to deliver on all their early promise and all their early hype and come up with a killer début album. In December 1979 they entered the studios.

CHAPTER FIVE

THE MEN WHO FELL TO EARTH

Def Leppard had hired Stirling Studios in Ascot, Berkshire, to the west of London and not far from the famous race course. Nick Tauber had been the man behind the control board for their only other release on the Vertigo label, the 'Wasted' single which some felt to be less than representative of their work. The man assigned the task of harnessing Def Leppard's obvious potential on to tape was 'Colonel' Tom Allom. Allom is perhaps best known, in Heavy Rock circles at least, for the continuously high standard of his work with Judas Priest. Allom produced no fewer than eight Priest albums. He also did much of his production and mixing work at Stirling so knew the lie of the land well.

The album was recorded in a matter of weeks and they finished on 5th January 1980. However, they barely had time to stretch their muscles and taste the joys of a 'normal' life once again before they were launched on a major UK tour that was to drag out over a gruelling sixteen weeks taking in well over fifty dates. The first dates of the tour were played in small clubs of a capacity of perhaps not more than a few hundred people. They were supported by other, lesser-known – and, it has to be said, lesser-talented – acts drawn from the 'New Wave of British Heavy Metal' such as Witchfynde and the Tygers of Pan Tang, most of whom eventually faded from the scene.

By this time the idea of there being a 'New Wave' of Heavy

Metal bands emerging in Britain – as a kind of backlash, or at least *reaction*, to the continued onslaught of the punk bands – was gaining some credibility. More and more bands were springing up, donning the traditional denim and leather uniform of the genre, and taking to the boards. The movement received impressive coverage – though, significantly, not to the same degree of *saturation* that the punk movement garnered – in the music press, particularly in *Sounds*, which could boast its own guru in Geoff Barton, whose rabid enthusiasm for the music was an influential factor in gaining it acceptance. The record companies, too, had noted the arrival in the market place of a whole crop of fans, most of whom were still at school, who had money to spend on their favourite pastime, *headbanging*.

The headbangers caused some raised eyebrows in the national press, and even some concern amongst the medical journals, through their ritualized dancing to the outbreak of Heavy Metal music which included banging their heads against walls. Some hysterical journalists suggested this practice was in danger of reaching epidemic proportions and damaging to the fabric of walls the length and breadth of the country. Needless to say the walls survived. Parents, meanwhile, were outraged as if a new kamikaze craze was about to snatch their children into oblivion. In reality, 'air guitars' were far more common as Heavy Metal discos opened to satisfy the needs of the thousands of fans nationwide who either couldn't see enough gigs or, more likely, couldn't afford to.

But what was perhaps more worrying was the record companies' reluctance to meet this obviously untapped market. Doubtless like the movement itself this was a cautionary reaction to the furore of the punk explosion. Many companies got their fingers burnt in a frenzy of deal-signing after the Sex Pistols had been snapped up and they were less than anxious to repeat the mistake they had made then – signing up any band because they looked like the Pistols only then to discover they couldn't sing, couldn't play, and couldn't make a record. The cream of the

'NWOBHM' crop had already been skimmed off the top: Saxon had their deal with Carrere before the 'New Wave' gained prominence; Motorhead had been taken on by Bronze Records, largely because of the presence of former Hawkwind star Lemmy Kilmister, and made some significant impact with their 1979 album *Overkill* – but then Motorhead always have been a band that stood out on their own, detached from the workings of any specific *movement*; Iron Maiden had been signed to EMI at the end of 1979; and now, of course, Def Leppard had their deal.

No one was taking any chances and all eyes, at least all of the A&R men's eyes, were centred on Def Leppard. Def Leppard had been the first band to create any real buzz within the industry and had almost single-handedly focused attention on this 'New Wave' of Heavy Metal. They were then crowned kings of the 'NWOBHM' pack while Iron Maiden lurked menacingly close, ready at any moment to step in and assume the throne. They wouldn't have to wait long.

With that position came an awful responsibility, one the band never asked for and never sought. The record companies waited, held off signing up anybody else, until they could see just what impact Def Leppard would make. Perhaps they weren't *really* convinced a market existed at all. They wanted figures, sales figures, and Def Leppard's début album would provide them with just that. So the world of Hard Rock waited with bated breath. This reluctance on the record companies' part to back the Heavy Metal 'New Wave' with hard cash in the form of deals was perhaps an ominous portent for Def Leppard who not only became the movement's first champions but also its first victims. Too much importance, too much responsibility was placed on their shoulders. Up till now their ride to success had seemed sweeter than any fairy tale. Everything had gone right for them in the two short years it had taken them to climb up the ladder of fame from their dingy Sheffield rehearsal room to national prominence as the forerunners of an exciting new musical pack. But what everyone failed to appreciate was that the *real* success lay in the effectiveness of the Def Leppard hype and now, as Frank Stuart-Brown had predicted, they were about to suffer all the indignities of over-exposure.

The problem with the Def Leppard phenomenon was that, essentially, it was constructed over a shallow hype and that in terms of sheer hard graft, of experience in the harsh world of rock 'n' roll, Def Leppard had actually achieved very little. Prior to the Sammy Hagar excursion Def Leppard had never actually undertaken a proper tour; they hadn't even done that many gigs! What they did have going for them was the fact that they were undoubtedly fine musicians with a great collection of songs – some of which were already being heralded as Heavy Metal classics alongside the likes of 'Smoke On The Water' and 'Paranoid' – and all this fronted by the imposing figure of frontman Joe Elliott, the cocksure ex-van driver who had great presence on stage.

No rock 'n' roll band ever made it without at least *one* visually commanding member and, partly by virtue of his tall, broad frame, Joe was certainly Def Leppard's most visual performer. Despite the importance of the twin-lead guitars to Def Leppard's music, though, neither Steve Clark nor Pete Willis came over as strongly as Joe, although of the two, Steve was certainly the more energetic. Pete was more introvert by nature and was even known, on occasion, to quit the stage altogether, preferring instead to play from behind the concealing security of his amps! This lack of self-confidence may have been part of the problem that led to his leaving the band to be replaced by the considerably more extrovert and ebullient Phil Collen. Steve, meanwhile, was travelling a rather slower route to the exit.

Def Leppard were still fairly new to the business of putting a band on the road for any length of time. Mistakes were made by all concerned. The tour manager was equally short of actual experience as he was drummer Rick's brother, Rob Allen, who had grown up with the band, becoming their first roadie, humping gear and driving them to and fro from gigs in his van.

His involvement made it natural enough that he should graduate to full blown 'tour manager' but inevitably, as with any organization, there were problems from time to time. On one occasion a number of hotel bookings were cancelled by somebody at the last moment leaving the band far from home and with nowhere to sleep! In themselves, these were hardly major disasters but to the band at the time they could sometimes seem like near apocalyptic catastrophes! These teething problems may also have contributed to the increasing rift between the band and the management, then Frank Stuart-Brown and Peter Martin.

Def Leppard had spent the beginning of the previous year writing and arranging new material to extend their repertoire in preparation for their first big break while Stuart-Brown and Martin were pounding the streets of London attempting to get them that break. So by the time the Sammy Hagar and AC/DC tours came round they had ample material to show off their songwriting skills and everyone was clearly impressed. Now, however, the time had come for them to go out and prove they could do it on their own!

But by now Def Leppard were beginning to swim against the tide and it appeared, at least from the outside, that the band were in a process of *re*gression instead of the *pro*gression they should have been making after the success of their autumn touring. As Frank Stuart-Brown had feared, were the band he had sold to the world as a major act of near-headlining status in fact, at this stage in their career, only capable of playing the clubs and not the big concert halls at all?

Of course the truth of the matter was somewhat different from the actual presentation – something that was to continue to dog the progress of Def Leppard's career in the home country for some time to come. The band doubtless *could* have set out on a major concert hall tour later in the year after the release of the début album, *On Through The Night*, perhaps after playing some small selective club dates as warm-ups. But the success of their EP, the signing with Phonogram, and the subsequent support slots on two major tours were still fresh in the memories of both the fans and the record industry. The spotlight was still very much on Def Leppard as they entered the studio to record their first album and remained there when they embarked on their first proper UK tour at the beginning of the new year. And what that spotlight revealed was a young band who were perhaps not as big as they had been perceived by some to be. This was no fault of Def Leppard, far from it, but no one likes to admit they have been taken in. Def Leppard were being forced to do their rock 'n' roll apprenticeships – to 'pay the dues' expected of any band – out there in the open before the public gaze and scrutiny. This really was their growing up in public.

Everything had gone *so* well up till then that Def Leppard really found themselves unprepared for the vehemence of the backlash that was to come their way, reaching its climax in August of that year when Leppard appeared at the annual Reading Festival. They might have had justifiable cause to shake their heads and wonder, 'Why us?' In reality it was simply a case of timing and circumstances working against them.

They had estimated that they'd played before some 40,000 people over the space of their two previous tours when interest/curiosity over just who this band whose EP was dominating the airwaves actually *were*, was at its height. But now that curiosity had been sated, everybody knew who Def Leppard were and most had gone away satisfied with what they'd seen. And now, barely two months after the AC/DC tour had closed, the same fans were being asked to fork over *more* money to see the *same* band, only this time in considerably less salubrious surroundings. For some this was simply too much to ask. In general things did not turn out as blackly as Frank Stuart-Brown had previously predicted, at least for the first half of the tour while they were still in the clubs; clubs like London's Marquee Club or Nottingham's Boat Club, small, sweaty, but intimate environments particularly suited to the energetic style of a band like Def Leppard engaged in a blitz situation. But if the idea was to reach more people, to get themselves better known by the crowd they hoped would turn into Def Leppard fans, the operation was only partially successful.

The end of February saw the release of the second Leppard single, 'Hello America', a record as beset with problems as the first, 'Wasted', had been. 'Hello America' had also been on the B-side of the 'Wasted' single. By now, of course, they'd re-recorded the song with Tom Allom. But apparently not all of the advertisements taken out for the release made this apparent nor made it clear enough that the B-side, a track called 'Good Morning Freedom', would not be available on the forthcoming album for which this release was obviously intended as a trailer. Had Phonogram begun to dictate the course of Def Leppard's career in such a way that they were overriding what the band themselves felt to be in their own, and their fans', best interests? Def Leppard *had* wanted to release 'Rock Brigade' as a single; just by virtue of its title it was a rockier, raunchier song closer to the hearts of both band and audience, though obviously with fewer commercial possibilities than 'Hello America'. 'Hello America' itself had long been included in Def Leppard's stage set showing the 'poppier' side to the band's rounded musical capabilities but was no less a Def Leppard song for all that. However, the decision to release this track as a single, against the – admittedly rather muted – wishes of the band, was a contributory factor in the growing suspicion amongst the music press that the band were 'selling out' to America, preparing at any moment to abandon the rain-drenched streets of Britain for the sunny climes of Beverly Hills. Nothing could have been further from the truth – but that's never stopped the press before!

The single was panned in *Sounds*, the reviewer coming tantamount to claiming that the Leppards had sold their souls to the rock 'n' roll industry. Another media blitz had been organized, meanwhile, only this time under the controlling hand of the Phonogram press office. The *Melody Maker* afforded them a full three-page spread written by noted Heavy Metal hater, Alan Jones. Jones did his best to send Def Leppard up, aided by

Steve's extreme case of drunkenness, but Joe managed to keep order. A few weeks later *Sounds* went one better by running Def Leppard on the cover, their first front cover of any periodical. But the piece inside, scripted once again by prime Def Leppard press champion, Geoff Barton, was a considerable leap away from the hysteria of his previous feature. The cover line ran 'Has the Leppard changed its spots?' with Barton arguing his concerned case that his discovery had allowed themselves to be overrun by the record industry and mourned for the independence they had once had on their own Bludgeon Riffola Records.

But all was not gloom and despondency in that issue of *Sounds* for the Leppards. They only had to flip back a page to see their name appear no less than twice. Not only had they scooped the 'Best New Band' category in the readers' poll results for the previous year – this, though, was hardly a surprising result considering the coverage *Sounds* had afforded them in the past – but also, staggeringly enough, the *Getcha Rocks Off* EP was voted into top place in the 'Best Single' category. While to gain 'Best New Band' they pipped other 'NWOBHM' contenders like Iron Maiden, Saxon, and Samson as well as Two-Tone acts like The Specials and Madness, to achieve top polling in the singles they'd managed to fend off smash-hits like Pink Floyd's 'Another Brick in the Wall', The Police's 'Message in a Bottle', and Tubeway Army's 'Are Friends Electric', alongside other more established Metal acts like Rainbow, Motorhead, and The Scorpions. It was an achievement of which they could be justifiably proud, perhaps even astounded, and surely this meant that, though the press might be giving them something of a rough ride, at least the fans were still on their side.

But this was to be their last glimmer of encouragement from the press for some time to come and also their last indication that they had strong fan support for some while, too. Before long the fans, largely misled and misguided by the press, would turn on the band too . . . and that was something the band really couldn't understand and was a reaction that hurt them very deeply. Then how did they score so well in that poll? Quite simply because the votes cast in the poll, like those in the *Melody Maker* and *NME* polls, were entered prior to the about-turn by the press, when it was still heavily behind Def Leppard. If anyone ever doubted the power and influence of the music press in Britain they need only ask Def Leppard for confirmation of their worst fears.

But Def Leppard had undoubtedly made a huge impact on the music scene in 1979, and that was part of the trouble. Their impact was *so* big too much was expected of them. After all, most of them were barely twenty years old and Rick had hardly left school! But the critics are always loath to take such mitigation into account when passing judgement, and the fans, whose money it is which actually supports both rock stars and journalists alike, still less.

Throughout March the Def Leppard tour moved into top gear, forsaking the clubs and taking to the concert halls. Once again Def Leppard were a *big* band and as the fans tended to come in their hundreds rather than their thousands the criticism began to filter through that maybe this was a band who'd had greatness thrust upon them rather than being born to it, and that maybe they really couldn't handle it. It was rather like the case of the New York Dolls and their prophetic album title, a case of *Too Much Too Soon*. They were also accused of lacking identity and any real sense of direction, and in short, of being almost a *manufactured* band constructed from every time-honoured Heavy Metal cliché in the book coupled with a sprinkling of all the most commercially successful Heavy Metal bands of the '70s.

Def Leppard, for their part, must have begun to wonder just what was going wrong. As far as they were concerned nothing had changed except that now they were playing bigger halls to bigger audiences. And wasn't that what was supposed to happen? Their set had scarcely changed, their personnel and presentation remained the same, they still played with the same force, drive, and exceptional musicianship as they had always tried to deliver. So what was going wrong?

A few weeks after they had scooped the two lead positions in the *Sounds* poll, their début album, *On Through The Night*, was released. Geoff Barton, despite giving it four stars (out of a possible five), then proffered a lukewarm review. Conversely, the *Melody Maker* raved, likening it to Van Halen's first album! This was well wide of the mark and even Joe – who co-wrote all the songs on the album – was three years later prompted to declare that the album was 'a load of shit'! But this judgement seems unduly harsh.

The plain fact is that *On Through The Night* remains, to this day, a *good* album. But what the world was waiting for in the spring of 1980 was a *great* album, and *On Through The Night* simply wasn't it. The album had its moments of greatness – or, to be more precise, moments that showed that there was true greatness *to come* – in such songs as 'It Could Be You' and a steaming live version of 'Rocks Off' (now having ditched the 'Getcha' from the title) but in the end it merely added fuel to the fire of the argument that Def Leppard were *Too Much Too Soon* casualties. In fact it was quite the reverse: it was the critics who expected *Too Much Too Soon* from Def Leppard and it certainly must have seemed from their side of the fence as if these critics were queueing up, licking their lips and waiting for the band to make their first slip.

On Through The Night was seen not so much as a slip as more a head-over-heels tumble. For a start there was the cover. The Leppards had originally wanted Hipgnosis, the artist/ designers who had created such stunning covers for acts like UFO, Led Zeppelin, Pink Floyd, and Leppard label-mates 10CC. But, once again, the record company organized the art- work using a less well-known and perhaps therefore cheaper artist called Melvin Smith. The result was in the view of some a tacky, lacklustre affair that succeeded in making the band look cheap. It depicted a diesel truck, motoring out into orbit around a pale, cheesy coloured moon, bearing a huge guitar as its load. Significantly enough, the truck also bears an American-style licence plate.

Inside, on the actual vinyl, matters hardly improved. Of the eleven tracks included no fewer than *four* had been previously available in one form or another. And one of those four tracks, 'Hello America', now made its *third* appearance on vinyl under Def Leppard's name.

And then one of the most serious criticisms levelled at the album was that of its production. 'Colonel' Tom Allom had been chosen, presumably, because of his heavyweight credentials. But even so *On Through The Night* somehow seemed to lack the edge and aggression that made the *Getcha Rocks Off* EP such an out-and-out classic.

Barton didn't actually say it *himself* but he reported one of his *colleagues* as saying that *On Through The Night* sounded as if it had been specifically made for an American audience. And indeed this was the overall impression, of an album that, at least production-wise, seemed geared towards the rather sanitized needs of American FM radio. Again, this really wasn't Def Leppard's fault although ultimately every band has to accept the responsibility for product that goes out bearing its name.

Def Leppard were as inexperienced in the studio as they were on the road; although by the time the second album came out it was clear they had learnt their lesson, and learnt it well. Their only *real* previous experience in a studio had been with Nick Tauber, the sessions that produced the first single. In replacing Tauber with Tom Allom the Leppards made several quantum leaps in the right direction to find the sound they were searching for as truly their own. At times the influences are rather too obvious on *On Through The Night* – Rush, for instance, on 'Overture' and 'When The Walls Come Tumblin' Down', or Judas Priest on 'Rock Brigade' and 'Answer To The Master' – which gave rise to criticism that they lacked direction. And they should have been safe enough with Allom at the control desk, given his pedigree, but perhaps there was a lack of communication or understanding between band and producer. When the final product of their labours emerged on vinyl, to many it just wasn't the *great* album Def Leppard wanted or, more to the point, *needed* at that stage in their career.

Even so, despite the fact that *On Through The Night* was an album beset by problems, despite the fact that it fell short of the remarkably high standards the band had set for themselves (or had had set for them, depending on which way you looked at it), and despite the fact that it was an opportunity they should have made more of, the album *still* charted highly on both sides of the Atlantic, reaching Number 11 in the UK album charts and Number 51 in the States. No mean achievement, certainly, for a band just beginning their career in earnest.

Nevertheless, the seeds of doubt had been planted by an increasingly vitriolic press in the minds of Def Leppard fans or, worse still, 'potential' Def Leppard fans. Didn't the album sound like it was made for an American audience rather than for the fans back home who had supported the band up till now? And what about that single, 'Hello America'? Wasn't that a clear indication of the intentions the band had – to quit Britain for the luxury of America just as soon as possible?

Rick Savage later said of 'Hello America': 'I listen to "Hello America" and I cringe . . . I just can't stand listening to it because the lyrics and the whole atmosphere of the song is so *Americanized* and we didn't know what then! Joe had just got these lyrics about America and we just decided to stick them in this song! But we were so naïve we didn't realize the implications of it. But looking back now I think: "Why did we ever do *that*?" We can see *now* that people will pick up on things like that but at the time we didn't realize.'

But then, as the Austrian-American film director Billy Wilder put it, 'hindsight is always 20/20', and Leppard can now see their mistakes sharply. But at the time people certainly did 'pick up on' it and the seemingly inevitable progress of the band was shaken. America, it seemed, beckoned to Def Leppard with the promise of streets paved with gold discs and the band appeared, at least from the outside, only too ready and willing to answer that call.

Then, with their UK tour behind them by the end of April, Def Leppard did exactly what everyone feared and suspected they would – they packed their bags and left for America. This, of course, was the right, sensible, and logical next step for them to make. With an album released there and doing well and, as far as they could gather, their commitment to Britain fulfilled by their extensive touring, shifting their attention, however temporarily, across the Atlantic was the correct thing to do. It made sound commercial sense too with the chance of opening for the Motor-City-Madman, Ted Nugent, who'd always proved himself a good box-office draw even though his album sales had been dropping off over the previous couple of years.

The States certainly looked like it was primed to extend a welcoming hand to Def Leppard and they were equally primed to accept the challenge offered. The difference was they weren't abandoning Britain for America's fairer climes as everyone back home seemed only too eager to believe. They weren't turning their backs on their home-country. Far from it, it was simply a question of Leppard realizing they had done everything they could reasonably be expected to do in Britain and now wanting to extend the horizons of their success. It was a brave move – especially considering how relatively inexperienced Leppard still were – but it wasn't seen that way at home and it cost the band dear.

Instead of seeing the trip to America for what it was – i.e. a trail-blazing expedition into the unknown by a young band which served to open the door for those coming up behind them (like Saxon and Iron Maiden) and showing America that the best Heavy Rock was still alive and kicking and flying the Union Jack – the description bandied about loosely and without any real basis in fact was: *sell out!* Def Leppard were being accused of selling out to America at the expense of Britain. And this was the worst possible criticism that could be levelled at them, particularly since it was so blatantly untrue and unfair.

Sell out is perhaps the most heinous crime any rock band can commit in the eyes of its fans, at least as far as British fans are concerned. Britain is really the only country in the world where divisions between musical categories are quite so rigidly enforced. There is quite a history of this splitting into factions throughout British Rock since its earliest beginnings: Mods v. Rockers, Skinheads v. Punks, even Beatles v. Rolling Stones, the divisions have always been there.

Part of the reason music has always been so strong in Britain is the fanatical loyalty it inspires from its followers, and there is none more frantic than the followers of Heavy Rock. Heavy Rock fans are generally loathed and reviled by everyone for being outmoded, ignorant, cliché-ridden, sheeplike; the list of criticisms and complaints is endless, some justified, many not. But the one thing Heavy Rock fans are, above all else, is intensely loyal to their heroes. It's a communal thing and doubtless a sociologist would have a field day exploring the roots of it all – if such a study hasn't already been undertaken somewhere – but in essence it's what has kept Heavy Rock alive and thriving for all these years.

Fashions come and go – and on occasion even Heavy Rock has been considered *fashionable* – but the music just carries on, progressing certainly, but its basic tenets remain very much intact. And that is part of its joy, that this third generation of Heavy Rock bands – the 'NWOBHM' – were playing a brasher, more developed form of rock than the first-generation bands – Cream, Deep Purple, Black Sabbath, etc. – but it was still very much built along the same lines. That lineage was recognizable, or rather *audible*, and the family of Heavy Rock fans grew up with everyone sharing a common heritage. This unity gives the fans and the bands their strength. And the loyalty is reciprocal. The fans continue to buy the albums and go to the gigs no matter how much they are derided in the media. And the bands, for their part, continue to provide the entertainment and musical excellence expected of them, again, in spite of the derision heaped upon them from all sides of the media. It's a kind of tribal thing and each side of the coin, the fans and the bands, keeps its pact with the other in a kind of grand 'Us against Them' campaign. But each side must be seen to keep their faith with the other. So when a Heavy Rock band gets accused of selling out it's a very serious charge. It means not just disloyalty to all the fans who supported them along the way, it means betrayal of everything those fans ever stood for. And having been betrayed, having breached that unwritten contract, these fans are loath to forgive a transgressor. And Def Leppard, so it appeared, had just transgressed!

Whatever the rights and wrongs of the situation, the plain fact remained that Def Leppard seemed to the fans back home to have sold out to America. That's what the papers said and that's what they believed. Whatever Def Leppard actually did or did not do thereafter became immaterial. If any of these fans could have been transported over to America to see Def Leppard perform they'd have borne witness that the only 'selling out' going on was at the box office and that the band were roaring through the country proving that Britain was still very much the home of Heavy Metal.

For while the storm clouds gathered back home across the water, Def Leppard were whipping up their own kind of storm! Playing half-hour sets prior to Ted Nugent hitting the stage, they were unleashing their own blistering twin-lead guitar attacks and bringing the roof down every night and even causing the stage to be rushed by ecstatic fans. For total unknowns they were going down better than anyone could have dreamed possible, most of all themselves. Considering their lack of experience and their brief on-stage time, the Leppards were simply thrown back on what they knew best: songs, musicianship, and a sense of fun. And that didn't escape an audience more used to a separation between band and fan. Here was a young act putting on a party and America seemed only too happy to join in, taking to the Sheffield lads like returning prodigal sons. Def Leppard set about repaying the compliment with thanks, playing better than they had ever done in their lives.

While in Britain the Leppards were tumbling rapidly and ignominiously to Earth, in America they were shooting for the stars. Aided by their fabulous success on the Ted Nugent tour *On Through The Night* climbed the *Billboard* chart just failing to make it into the Top 50. Already Def Leppard were stars. And all this was achieved in a matter of just eleven short weeks!

Winding up the tour the band returned to Britain at the beginning of August to spend two or three weeks rehearsing and writing some more new material. For they had received even greater news: they were to play second on the bill to the hugely popular Whitesnake at the Reading Festival, Europe's largest outdoor music event. If they had only known what lay in store for them, though, they might well have wished they had sold out and never come home at all.

CHAPTER SIX

GIMME SHELTER

Officially the Reading Festival was titled the 'National Jazz, Blues and Rock Festival' but the jazz element had disappeared entirely and the blues put in only occasional appearances. It was a rock festival and had been for many years. It was held on a regular site just outside the town centre of Reading on the banks of the River Thames, some forty miles west of London in the county of Berkshire. It was something of an institution before its backers, London's famous Marquee Club, pulled out in the 1980s and before it was resurrected under the management of another London venue, the Mean Fiddler.

In 1980 the Reading Festival was celebrating its twentieth year; sadly, it was to prove its most troubled. The festival remained a prestige event, held over three days on the last weekend in August, which coincides with a national public holiday in the UK. On each of the three days around 30,000 people would attend, making it the largest music festival in Europe and also one of the most successful. To play the Reading Festival was a coveted prize and positioning on the bill was, generally, a firm indicator of a band's status in the rock field. But sometimes it did not work out like this.

1980 was the year the Reading Rock Festival was blitzed – some might say assailed and beleaguered – by Heavy Metal. That year the festival finally gave irrefutable proof of the revived fortunes of the Heavy Metal market and the so-called 'New Wave Of British Heavy Metal' was prominently featured amongst the bill alongside some of the rather older statesmen of rock. Indeed, it was almost a case of 'If you weren't on the Reading bill that year, you weren't anyone!'

The weekend line-up included Samson, Grand Prix, White Spirit, Praying Mantis, Angelwitch, The Tygers of Pan Tang, Sledgehammer, and Girl, who featured the dapper-dressed and Britt Ekland-dated singer called Phil Lewis who would later front LA Guns, and a diminutive blond guitarist by the name of Phil Collen. They played to the assembled throng over the course of the three days, scattered in amongst more established artists like Whitesnake, UFO, Pat Travers, Budgie, and Slade.

In recognition of their prominence in the field Def Leppard were accorded the second-on-the-bill slot for the Sunday night. Iron Maiden, meanwhile, had shot to fame with a hit single and album – 'Running Free' and *Iron Maiden* – and some smart and gimmicky publicity garnered courtesy of their 'mascot', the ghoulish Eddie. Eddie was a ridiculous, almost skeletal figure who graced their record sleeves and even appeared on stage with the band under the guise of a roadie and the appropriate props and make-up. Eddie was a huge favourite with the crowds and one of the most memorable events of that year's Reading Festival was seeing the Iron Maiden roadies, each decked out in eight-foot Eddie costumes – normally it was just the one Eddie! – laying siege to the stage at the close of the band's set.

Since signing to EMI in December 1979 Iron Maiden had challenged Def Leppard's leadership of the 'New Wave' and at Reading they snatched the crown away from the Sheffield boys altogether. To some musically inferior to Leppard, Iron Maiden still managed to retain their 'street credibility' – a nebulous but none the less crucial attribute for any band in those days – due largely to their singer Paul Di'Anno's decidedly 'punky' image. He was short-haired and leather-jacketed and looked like a tough, street-wise kid. He also lent the band an earthy quality that stood out in direct contrast to the Def Leppard approach.

Curiously, this image remained steadfast when Di'Anno was replaced by the far more flamboyant former Samson lead singer, Bruce Dickinson. Leppard, though, had always tried to put on a show for their fans and that included dressing up and looking the part, hence the leather jeans, the spandex-and-satin image. Conversely, Iron Maiden really looked like they'd just stepped in off the street and on to the stage, as all good punk bands were supposed to do. Maiden also played a far more basic form of Heavy Metal than Leppard ever did and, consequently, when the cries of 'sell out' reverberated around Def Leppard over their American tour and their supposedly *Americanized* music, many fans turned for solace to Iron Maiden to supply them with the true-blue, very *British* form of rock they sought. And Iron Maiden were quite happy to deliver.

It is interesting to record that Iron Maiden began to take off in America only after Di'Anno had gone and, with the acquisition of Dickinson, the band started to shape up their image considerably. The leather jackets remained but otherwise they took several lessons from the Leppards in their style of dress. And, on the Saturday night when Iron Maiden played in the same slot to UFO as Leppard did to Whitesnake the following day, they found themselves several notches up the pecking order from Samson, who featured Bruce Bruce on vocals. Dickinson, presumably, did not attach much 'street-credibility' to his surname; by the time he hitched up with Iron Maiden the second 'Bruce' had been dropped.

While Iron Maiden, who hailed from the East End of London, were at home touring the country as support to Judas Priest or playing their own shows, snapping up fans wherever they went, their chief rivals, Def Leppard, had 'deserted' Britain in favour of an American tour. The fans were being told by the press they'd 'sold out', and when they appeared at Reading, the contrast with Iron Maiden only seemed to confirm that suspicion. Result: Iron Maiden emerged as the new heroes of British Heavy Metal and Def Leppard were left to lick their wounds.

The other type of metal on display that year at the festival was the tin can, which flew in abundance, sometimes towards the bands on stage, more often simply from one part of the audience to another. There were times that year when the sky seemed black with cans and some bands were even forced off stage by the deluge of missiles hurled at them by a dissatisfied audience. In fact so bad did this downpour of cans become that the organizers banned them from all future events. But in 1980 it seemed no power on Earth could prevent the Metal fans from venting their anger at any miscreants unfortunate enough to appear before them on the stage. It was not a time for the faint-hearted.

On the Saturday Iron Maiden gave a triumphant perform-ance prior to headliners UFO taking the stage. But twenty-four hours later things did not go so smoothly. Earlier in the afternoon those other 'snappy dressers' of the 'NWOBHM' movement, Girl, were unceremoniously given the *can treatment* and forced to pare their set to a bare minimum. Then, going on just before Leppard, were Slade, who were in the process of engineering a come-back after years in the wilderness. Slade, whose greatest popularity had been during the early '70s as part of the Glitter Rock fad, became the heroes of the day. Slade were always the perfect festival band with their short, simple songs, singalong choruses, and larger-than-life characters set off by their ludicrous stage gear. They went down a storm, offering the Sunday crowd a party which, at that point, was exactly what was required. They eventually retired from the stage having set the ball rolling on their return to former glories. But they set Def Leppard an almighty hurdle to overcome. How could they possibly follow that?

Def Leppard were up there with the 'big boys', slotted in between the returning conquering heroes, Slade, and perhaps the weekend's biggest attraction, Whitesnake, who were riding on the success of a smash hit single, 'Fool For Your Loving', and the album, *Ready an' Willing*, released earlier in the year. It was surely the most unenviable spot of the entire weekend and, coupled with all the adverse publicity they'd encountered during their absence from home, they simply became offered up like lambs to the sacrificial slaughter on the altar of Reading Festival. But, of course, as they prepared to go on stage they didn't have any clue what lay in store for them.

Def Leppard were still bubbling from the sensational response they'd been afforded at the hands of their new, and blossoming, American audience. They brimmed with confidence as they sought to entertain the 30,000 Metal fans before them. It was to be a humbling experience.

With all the stories of American excesses spoiling the Sheffield lads they were not likely to be greeted, as they perhaps in reality deserved to be, as the latest in a long line of trail blazers for the British Metal cause across the continent of America. But if anyone in that audience had been prepared to give Leppard the benefit of the doubt the sight of Joe Elliott must surely have dispelled any lingering doubts, cementing their doom. In the early evening of that balmy August day, Joe had decided to sport his slickest New York get-up. He wore a light white jacket over a white T-shirt strewn with pink hearts. But the hearts in the audience were not captured by such extravagance. Remember, leather jackets and jeans were the standard Heavy Metal uniform and T-shirts with pink hearts were definitely not what was required. So it was true, and there was the proof, Def Leppard *had* sold out. Not only had he spurned the denim-and-leather – as, in fact, he always had done, but such minor details are quickly forgotten in the heat of the moment – but he also carried with him an all too prominent paunch, more positive proof of what tales the press had been telling of their hedonistic existence across the Atlantic. And so the seal was set and the cans came thundering down on Def Leppard.

Def Leppard might have looked for some sympathy, or even a fair chance to be heard, but there were no favours to be gained that evening and, despite playing a fine set backed by an extremely impressive light show, the best they could hope for was to escape uninjured. Whitesnake were then left to bring the weekend to a victorious close while the debris was cleared from Def Leppard's stage. The former kings of the 'New Wave Of British Heavy Metal' were dethroned and banished into exile in the space of an afternoon.

The message to Def Leppard, then, was clear and quite simply they were left with no option. The British public, which had initially taken to them so enthusiastically, had now turned its back on them and rejected them out of hand. Def Leppard were forced to flee the country in confusion, taking off on a European tour where their fans were untainted by the music press claims of a 'sell out' and where they could still work unhindered on building up a following.

The implications of the Reading Festival débâcle were obvious and quite damaging: in front of 30,000 ardent Metal fans Def Leppard had come crashing down to Earth. For all the talk of their American successes and excesses the Leppards could still be seen to be both human and intensely vulnerable to the disfavour of the fans proving, at least to them, that they still had the power to make or break any band of their choice. It also gave the fans the satisfaction of dealing a retributive blow to a band they believed had somehow betrayed their common roots and their common cause. Justice, it must have seemed, was not only done but seen to be done!

Except, of course, that there was no justice in it. Their trail blazing for the new British Hard Rock in America was simply deemed to be selling out; songs that had long been part and parcel of their set and had once been hugely popular with their British fans were now seen as a deliberate attempt to woo American favour; even their style of dress, which had long set them apart from the dullness and drudgery of their competition, was looked upon as further evidence of their betrayal from their class and all it stood for.

So Def Leppard left their home and went to Europe to ponder just where it had all gone wrong. Where was the fairness in it all? Def Leppard could have been forgiven if, after this indignity, they had decided there and then to jack it all in and disappear into obscurity. But they were made of sterner stuff than that. From that point on, in the shadow of their treatment at the Reading Festival, Britain became a hurdle, a challenge – and an intensely *personal* one – that had to be overcome. Cracking Britain, thereafter, became a matter of pride for Def Leppard.

Over the next couple of years, as their success in America sky-rocketed, they would turn their eyes longingly towards Britain, aching for the same kind of acceptance there that Iron Maiden enjoyed courtesy of their ardent and fanatical following. They would also return as often as possible from their lucrative foreign tours, particularly the American ones, which continued to be real money-spinners, in order to place themselves in front of the British public for their scrutiny and, hopefully, their ultimate approval. It would prove a long and arduous struggle, not to mention an extremely expensive one. Touring the UK has *never* been a viable commercial proposition for any band save the few stadium-fillers like Led Zeppelin, the Rolling Stones, U2, or Madonna. The most a band could hope for from a UK tour would be to break even, itself a rather exceptional event. But on their side Def Leppard counted strength of character and determination that would never receive a greater test.

Meantime, Europe offered them solace and shelter through September and in October they slipped back into the country to begin work on the follow-up album to *On Through The Night*.

CHAPTER SEVEN

FAME

If 1980's Reading Festival was a test of Def Leppard's strength of character then what was to follow their return to Britain at the end of their European jaunt was to test their stamina even further. Patience is a virtue, but Def Leppard practically needed to be saints to come through their up-coming ordeal. Spirits were at their lowest ebb and in such situations most artists find the most therapeutic activity work and lots of it. Def Leppard, doubtless, would have loved to have thrown themselves into their work . . . the only trouble was they had no work in which conveniently to throw themselves.

The life of a rock band from the outside – and especially to their fans – looks very glamorous and, in truth some of it *is* spectacularly beguiling. But, away from the shows and the parties and the cameras, it takes on the same mundanity and ordinariness of any other perfectly 'normal' job in its relentless, year-in, year-out progression. An album is written, rehearsed, recorded, rehearsed for the road, and finally toured. While on tour the band may write some of the material to be used on the next album. Then, following perhaps a short break, a new album is written and the whole process starts all over again. To a rock band this is the most natural and regular sequence of events they will know. With both touring and recording in particular usually being night-time activities this lifestyle can be quite disorienting. While fans may dream of the excitement and glamour of life on the road, bands too often dream of the same normal, ordered life their fans want to escape. It always looks greener on the other side.

The trouble, as far as Def Leppard were concerned at the end of 1980, was that that chain, that commonplace sequence of events, had been broken. What they should have been doing, if things had been working properly, was going into a studio and preparing and recording their new album. The problem? Simply that this time instead of being unable to find the right person to sit in the production chair to oversee the new project (they knew exactly who they wanted) they now couldn't use him.

This time round, the band were adamant, there would be no mistakes. They recognized the message given them embossed at the end of a tin can at Reading. That was the culmination of a series of events, most of which in themselves didn't appear to mean much at the time, that brought Leppard crashing down from the dizzy heights they scaled on the Sammy Hagar and AC/DC tours. The problems, the arguments, the niggling difficulties would have to stop if Def Leppard ever wanted to regain that lofty position they had once held in the eyes of fans all over the UK. This time they took charge and presented the fans with what they believed was an accurate representation of themselves – a real, honest, hard-working band who played hard rock like the best of them but with more melody packed in than most of their rivals could possibly hope to match. And they knew the man who they believed was best qualified to help them achieve that objective. His name was Robert John 'Mutt' Lange.

Today Mutt Lange is one of the most respected, and no doubt richest, rock producers in the world. He has worked with bands as disparate as The Boomtown Rats, Billy Ocean and AC/DC. Indeed it was his work in 1979 with the Australian rock band that first attracted Def Leppard to the sound he could create in a studio. Rick Savage explained: 'We wanted Mutt Lange to do the first album because we'd heard what he'd done on some of the AC/DC albums, especially *Highway To Hell* [released in 1979]. We would have used him, too, but he just wasn't available. He was right in the middle of doing another album and with it being the first one we couldn't exactly wait for him so we went ahead and did it with Tom Allom.

'When we'd finished the album Mutt got the chance to listen to it and he said: "Whenever you want to do the second album I'd like to produce it." So it was a two-way thing, he wanted to produce us and we *really* wanted him!'

In the band's view Mutt Lange was the man to bring out all the aggression and energy inherent in their music, which seemed to many to be lacking on their first album, while at the same time maintaining the melody and overall sophistication of their songs. What they were after, essentially, was an American *sound* with a British *edge*; the slickness of an American structure coupled with the raw brutality of a distinctly British attack. They wanted an album that would satisfy fans on both sides of the Atlantic, giving both what they wanted while still retaining their identity as Def Leppard.

To some it may have seemed an impossible task but the album that Mutt Lange was engaged in producing at that time might easily have served as a blueprint for exactly what Def Leppard were seeking. That record eventually, and after much delay and heartache, emerged as the smash hit 4 by Foreigner. The album was a blockbuster and set Foreigner off on a worldwide trek plugging their masterpiece for something like eighteen months, an extraordinary period even by rock-band standards. More importantly, to Def Leppard anyway, it broke Foreigner in Britain.

Foreigner were basically a British band, led by former Spooky Tooth guitarist Mick Jones with two other Englishmen comprising the rhythm section – Dennis Elliott (no relation) on drums and Rick Wills on bass – with only vocalist Lou Gramm being a native American. However, the band were based in the States and the common perception was that, to all intents and purposes, they *were* an American band. But for Leppard the trouble was that it was taking Mutt Lange so long to finish 4. And time was pressing.

Both Lange and Foreigner were tight-lipped about the reasons for the delay in completing the album, a delay that was to stretch over an incredible seven-month period and consequently cause further delay to the new Def Leppard album. In fact, so long was the wait for the Leppard follow-up album many people believed the band had simply slunk away in shame to disappear off the face of the Earth. The most commonly touted story was that Mick Jones, the chief composer as well as leader, had agreed with his wife that he would finish work at 5 p.m. after a 9 a.m. start and woe betide anyone who tried to interfere! Since most recording sessions rarely start before the afternoon this cannot have created an easy working environment especially if the most important member had to clock off every day at 5 p.m.! Then there were reports that Jones had fallen heavily under the influence of the sound created by his namesake in The Clash and had penned a load of Clash-style material that was totally unsuitable for a Foreigner album. He was then virtually forced to rewrite the entire album in the studio. Then again, maybe it was a combination of the two or even a totally different reason. Whatever, the main cause for concern was that it brought Def Leppard's activities crashing to a halt.

As they waited through October and into November of 1980 the pressure must have been on to change their minds and go with another producer since it looked as if Mutt Lange was heavily entrenched and without any real sign of the situation improving. Even though their frustration and feeling of helplessness must have been intense the Leppards stuck to their guns. They wanted Mutt Lange because, in their view, he was the best there was and they wanted nothing short of the best . . . even if they had to wait a long, long time.

And a long time it looked like being as November stretched into December and there still appeared to be no light at the end of the Foreigner tunnel. The band were becoming pinned down by their own inactivity and threatened by boredom. The pace at which most rock bands operate is so great that any extended period where they're not actually on the road or recording or rehearsing can be dangerous because of that looming spectre called 'boredom'. And Def Leppard were then very much at risk of falling victim to it and all its unhealthy consequences. They needed to get out and re-establish some contact with the people it seemed they'd left behind. They needed to get back to their roots.

So a small, very low-key tour of the UK was set up, just a few clubs so the band could keep their hand in, keep themselves together and relieve the stultifying boredom of just *waiting*! But things didn't work out like that, people weren't so quick to forget. Def Leppard were still being ostracized by the fans, they were still *personae non gratae*. And so *non gratae* were they the fans simply didn't turn up to the gigs in any numbers. They even had to cancel one gig because the advance tickets sales amounted to only a handful with no promise of any more turning up at the door on the night. Things were looking pretty desperate for Def Leppard and Christmas that year was not a particularly festive one.

So Def Leppard had to go back home, their tails between their legs, and do some more waiting as the New Year came round. They continued to wait through the remainder of the winter and into the spring. Finally, in May, seven months after Def Leppard had declared themselves ready to begin, Mutt Lange finally freed himself from Electric Ladyland Studios where he had been recording 4. Now, at last, work could begin in earnest.

The importance of this product couldn't be overestimated in terms of Def Leppard's career. In effect it was whether they had a future in rock 'n' roll or not. The choice was that simple and they knew it. The new album and its success or failure meant the make-or-break for Def Leppard; after this one there would be no more chances. They had played all their cards except this one, their last remaining trump, and now everything rested on this final play. If the album bombed – as, given the frosty reception they encountered on their December mini-tour, they might well have expected it to – that would be the end of Def

Leppard as any kind of force in the rock industry. If it succeeded they could begin to rebuild their tarnished stature from scratch, only this time based on an album of hard, solid rock rather than the hype that their initial rise to stardom had been constructed on.

Def Leppard were only too aware of just how much they had riding on this new album, just how much was really at stake. That's why they hung out for so long to ensure they secured the services of Mutt Lange, the only man they were convinced could drastically alter the plummeting course of their careers, the one man who could, if anyone could, make that vital difference.

So it was with something more than a little trepidation that they entered Battery Studios in North London in May 1981 to record *High 'n' Dry*. But the songs were right, they were certain, the material was strong and this time everything would go right.

The album was ready for release in July, by which time Def Leppard were already back on the road plugging the new material, where they would remain until the end of the year. And what material! Anyone who might have thought to dismiss Def Leppard as just another flash-in-the-pan band was instantly silenced by the sheer power of *High 'n' Dry*. Ten tracks portrayed Def Leppard, finally, as the band they really were! Raw, gutsy, energetic songs interspersed with softer, subtler ballads displaying every facet of the Leppard character to the fullest exposure. And all doubts were removed, the band performed awesomely and the key word to the project was definitely 'power'. It dripped from every pore, from the rip-roaring opening track, 'Let It Go', to the closing screams of 'No No No' – Def Leppard had delivered a masterpiece.

Its onslaught was formidable and from the opening chords of 'Let It Go' it was clear the band had moved into a different league from the one in which they had recorded the rather naïve *On Through The Night* two years before. 'Let It Go' had a big sound that positively dwarfed anything on their début album, pile-driven along by Rick Allen's drumming while the guitars raced and interwove. 'Another Hit and Run' continued the pattern before 'High 'n' Dry (Saturday Night)' crashed in with its defiant force. It could have been screamed from the football terraces, it cried out to anyone who cared to listen: 'This is what Def Leppard are all about, a good times rock 'n' roll band who are out for fun!' but this time stamped in an aggressive and determined manner. There was no 'sell out' about this band and *High 'n' Dry* was their way of proving it!

Side one closed with the ballad 'Bringin' On The Heartbreak' which segued into the Steve Clark composed instrumental 'Switch 625'. This number gave the band the chance to display their not inconsiderable musical muscle as well as their virtuosity. It was a bold statement and said much for the confidence Def Leppard were finding again in themselves through their music.

Side two continued in much the same vein with the band going full tilt through the rockers 'You Got Me Runnin'', 'On Through The Night', and 'No No No', finding more sensitive moments on 'Lady Strange' and almost verging into pomp with 'Mirror Mirror (Look Into My Eyes)' But the message of the album came storming through: Def Leppard were back and this time they *really* meant business. They proved beyond all doubt that they could rock out with the best of them as well as provide some gentler, subtler moments that many of their contemporaries found simply beyond them. *High 'n' Dry* found Leppard once again asserting themselves on the album battlefield when everybody had believed them dead and buried. It was a bold and brazen album and a clear statement that its makers were far from finished yet. This was their first step in their attempt to claw their way back to the top. It was, perhaps, only a foothold but it was a start and they couldn't have wished for a better send-off. They even got their Hipgnosis cover this time round!

Two singles were released from the album, 'Let It Go' and 'Bringin' On The Heartbreak', the latter in both 7" and 12" with an otherwise unavailable track, 'Me And My Wine', which is probably an outtake from the *High 'n' Dry* sessions as it is not one of Leppard's finer songs.

But of course by the time the album was issued in July Leppard were out treading the boards again ahead of it. They had already taken their show featuring the new songs through Europe supporting the flailing fortunes of Ritchie Blackmore's Rainbow, through Britain on a headlining – and, fortunately, rather better attended – tour before setting off across America on their most ambitious journey yet.

They began with a five-week tour supporting rock's resident madman, Ozzy Osbourne – itself always an eye-opening, not to mention at times *harrowing*, experience – as the album was released. They knew they'd given the project their best shot, got the best producer working on their best songs, but even the Leppards must have been surprised, even *stunned* perhaps, when the music press back home stopped hounding them and gave the album a unanimous thumbs-up. Yes, they agreed, it was a genuine scorcher! Def Leppard were at long last delivering on the potential they had promised so early in their career and the press seemed even prepared to forgive them all their previous 'misdemeanours'.

The band had come to recognize their earlier effort, *On Through The Night*, for what it was: a naïve if spirited attempt that didn't quite come off. Today they are more prepared to dismiss it altogether and cite, perhaps understandably, *High 'n' Dry* as the first *true* Def Leppard album, the first that really represented them and their music. Even so, *On Through The Night* provided some valuable ground work when it came to cracking the States.

Rock stations all across the country had picked up on the anthemic 'Rock Brigade' off the first album and this became a corner-stone from which the band could build. So when *High 'n' Dry* was released, with its far superior sound quality and production values, these same radio stations, and a whole host of others who correctly saw what was coming, were immediately much more receptive to the album. Def Leppard were fast becoming radio hits and that, in America anyway, generally translates into sales. By the time Def Leppard released their third album, *Pyromania*, *High 'n' Dry* had clocked up sales of over a million, awarding it platinum status, having stayed inside the *Billboard* Top 200 for an incredible one hundred weeks, reaching No. 38. It was an astonishing achievement for a band so young – particularly for a band who had been persecuted so vigorously at home – and it was to set the scene for the deluge to come.

With the album rocketing up the US charts, Def Leppard stayed on the Ozzy Osbourne tour opening for a total of five weeks, all the time getting more and more exposure, gaining more and more fans. And as the tour came to a halt they set off almost immediately, this time opening for Southern Boogie band Blackfoot, striking at the heart of America as forcefully and as comprehensively as possible. Ostensibly Def Leppard were the support act on the Blackfoot tour but it became increasingly clear over its eleven-week duration that the Leppards were drawing at least as many supporters into the halls as the main band, and towards the end of the tour it was being billed more as a 'co–headliner' than a traditional headline/support show with 'Def Leppard' appearing in as large a typeface as 'Blackfoot' wherever and whenever the concerts were advertised.

Def Leppard were becoming stars, that much was obvious, and the word began to filter back home; maybe everyone had been wrong about Def Leppard after all. Meanwhile, in the States, coinciding with the release of *High 'n' Dry*, came the opening broadcast of a new TV phenomenon called 'Music Television', MTV, the twenty-four-hour music video network. MTV helped break a number of British acts in America, Duran Duran and the Leppards' old Sheffield rivals The Human League among them. This was as much by accident as design, though. A TV picture and its definition is made up of a series of lines across the screen. The more lines there are, the higher the definition and the sharper the picture. American TV sets have considerably fewer lines than British sets do. So a video made for a UK system and then transferred for American broadcast always looks sharper and finer than the home-grown product. In short, the British videos just *looked* better! Add that to the fact that, to this day, Britain still leads the world in video production techniques and that when MTV started it simply didn't have *that* many videos to play, it was glad to broadcast anything new it could grab hold of – and British record companies were only too happy to oblige.

Given this, it's easy to see why *British* struck US TV viewers as *best*. So when Def Leppard issued the ballad 'Bringin' On The Heartbreak' as a single and MTV snapped up the accompanying video, its success was assured giving the album a further boost. With its high rotation play, 'Bringin' On The Heartbreak' not only saw Def Leppard emerging as stars but also as new 'teeny-bop' idols. It all seemed incredible, once again Def Leppard were experiencing a total turn-around in their fortunes and this time it was due in no small part to the fact that enough people had turned on to the new video station often enough for these clean-cut English boys to make an impression. And these were people who might not necessarily ever venture out to a rock 'n' roll gig. A whole new audience was opening up for them and this time they were making the most of it.

Their arduous US touring schedule finally came to a close in October but there could be no let up. Riding on the back of their staggering Stateside success the band flew straight back to Europe to tour with Judas Priest, still as the opening act. It must have felt strange to Steve and Pete Willis, playing now on the same stage as the band at whose gig they had forged their guitar partnership just a few years before at the Sheffield City Hall. Their lives had changed, and changed dramatically. They had at last found the fame they had striven for and, it had to be said, so richly deserved, as well as the accompanying musical accolades. They had become stars and were all the time gaining respect both as musicians and performers. But as their support slot on Judas Priest's European tour brought them to the end of 1981, for Pete Willis those glory days were also drawing to a close.

CHAPTER EIGHT

AMERICAN HOT WAX

In 1982 Def Leppard activity apparently ground to a complete halt. Once again the question eventually began to be asked: What *had* happened to Def Leppard? Just as it looked like they might be beginning to break through in a big way . . . suddenly nothing, no recognizable signs of activity, certainly no roadwork. So what *had* happened?

The answer was quite simple. The Leppards got themselves locked away in an assortment of studios with *High 'n' Dry* mega-producer Mutt Lange, attempting to come up with a product that would finally swing fortune their way. Unfortunately that project would drag on far longer than anyone anticipated and was, as had now become almost customary, beset with problems. However, the result of all their effort, craftsmanship, sweat, blood, and heartache would establish them as one of the greatest rock bands of the age and place them very firmly on the top of the pile, kings of all they surveyed! The result was an album called *Pyromania*.

Pyromania was to turn Def Leppard from a promising up-and-coming rock band into international superstars. The album delivered on all the promise *High 'n' Dry* had proved them capable of, silenced their critics, and became the turning point in their career. Although its recording was a long, arduous process and far from problem-free, it enabled Def Leppard finally to put their troubled past to rest, become free agents, and look to the future without the constant glancing-over-the-shoulder to see what new gremlin was creeping up behind them.

Pyromania was also something of a watershed in that it stopped people comparing Def Leppard to others bands – Led Zeppelin, Judas Priest, Rush, etc., etc. – and instead bands were now being compared to, and indeed trying to *sound like*, Def Leppard. Def Leppard were no longer the 'New Kids on the Hard Rock Block', instead they were the yardstick by which everybody else was now measured. In short, Def Leppard, through the medium of that one album, *Pyromania*, had made it. And this time they'd not only made it but made it *big*!

But it was not as easy road. *Pyromania* was an album dogged by delay after delay, sometimes totally beyond the band's control . . . other times not quite so far beyond. For instance, two whole weeks were lost due to Joe Elliott's recurring throat problem. And another couple of weeks of recording time were swept under the carpet while the 1982 World Cup soccer finals were played. Broadcast direct from Spain where England battled their way through the quarter final stage, every moment of the action was soaked up by the soccer-crazed Leppards. All thought of recording the most important album of their career was instantly dispelled in their all-consuming passion for their national sport! And even when England were eliminated they felt they had to watch the final rounds to their gory end with Italy triumphing 3–2 over West Germany, the 'safe bet' to win after the 'hot favourites', Brazil, had fallen from grace earlier on. It was riveting drama being played out there on the fields of Spain and Def Leppard, patriots to a man, didn't intend to overlook a single mis-kick of England's unsteady progress, and thereafter the Italians' even more erratic advance to the trophy.

So all recording was postponed and such was the sense of high drama gleaned from the entire tournament the band even felt compelled to mention it in the credits of the eventually completed album: 'Recorded between bouts of World Cup soccer' it reads. Quite what Mutt Lange's reaction to all this was, as a renowed perfectionist and stickler for the 'work ethic', has, sadly, slipped unrecorded into the fog of history.

The band would have felt that the World Cup was an 'unavoidable' delay, that it definitely took precedence over anything they might have been achieving in the studio that summer. It can fairly safely be assumed that the record company thought otherwise! But the other cause for delay – not to mention *concern*: Joe's throat really was down to the hand of fate. Part of the problem was psychological: the pressure to come up with an Earth-shattering album this time and the gruelling pace of the twelve hours a day spent in the studio – when they weren't watching the soccer.

The fact that this time Joe was really being stretched to the absolute limits of his ability by Mutt Lange contributed to the breakdown of his voice. So, while part of the problem was simply a reaction to the pressure, part of it was also this driving for perfection that Lange insisted on. Joe had never really rated himself *as* a singer, being a 'failed' drummer and guitarist prior to Def Leppard, and now he was being asked to perform feats of vocal gymnastics.

Joe, perhaps more than any other of his colleagues, had progressed the most as a musician and as a performer since the early days by the end of this process. This progress must, in a large part, be due to the way he was pushed by Mutt Lange to bring out the very best in himself during these sessions. The difference between the power of the vocals on the first album and *Pyromania* is very marked – the difference, in effect, between a young apprentice struggling to learn his trade and an accomplished performer having mastered the technique under some expert tuition.

But for some time it was touch-and-go and the strain began to make itself evident. Joe is not a 'natural' nor even a trained singer, by his own confession. Unlike Steve Clark, a classically taught guitarist, Joe had had no formal education as a vocalist. He just thumped it out as best he could relying on 'feeling' rather than 'technique' to carry him through. But this had earlier on in his career run him into trouble and now his voice just gave out completely.

Joe was packaged off to consult a vocal specialist in New York called Joe Scott, whose clients also numbered the Rolling Stones' Mick Jagger. Scott assured Joe that his 'technique', such as it was, was in fact correct but then ordered him to rest for two weeks. Joe returned to the fray with his troubles behind him, brimming with confidence, and polished off the remaining vocal tracks in the space of a week!

But that wasn't the only vocal problem Def Leppard experienced while recording *Pyromania*. Both the band and Mutt Lange decided they wanted Leppard to do their own backing vocals on the album. Normally these backing vocals are recorded by the lead singer and mixed in later; on occasion they are farmed out to guests or session musicians; but rarely are they attempted by the usually silent other band members. But they wanted to spend the time on this facet of their otherwise untested repertoire 'because there's nothing worse than hearing harmonies that you can tell are just the singer again!' And, once again under Lange's perfectionist hand, *time* was precisely what it took due to the fact that The Leppardettes – as they dubbed themselves – were not the best singers in the world. But eventually they succeeded in attaining something Lange found acceptable. And all the while time slipped inexorably away . . .

This jaunt into the previously unexplored world of backing vocals accounted for something like a month of recording time. And, in total, that recording time would stretch almost the entire length of 1982, clocking up an incredible ten months in an assortment of studios that finally numbered no less than *ten*. Despite this, most of the work was done in Battery Studios, near the town of Battle in Sussex, on the south coast of England, site of the Battle of Hastings in 1066. The *battle* here, though, was more along the lines of titanic guitar duels or thundering drum rolls, which was another of *Pyromania*'s continuing sound problems: getting the right drum sound. This difficulty consumed something like 'six to eight weeks . . . the weeks just came and went!'

And then there was the inordinately complicated tracking of some of the songs. '"Rock Of Ages" has got something like ninety-six tracks on it. Not exactly the kind of attitude a band like Iron Maiden would have, where they'd go into a studio and try to create a "live feel" there and then, exactly the opposite side of the coin to us.' For the uninitiated, most songs on albums are recorded over twenty-four tracks, with each instrument being given two or more tracks to create the rounded sound that eventually comes out of the speakers at home. In other words, Mutt Lange was employing four times as many tracks as normal to record some of the material here and achieve that 'perfect' sound.

Once again, it was Lange's insistence that *everything* about *Pyromania* be perfect that held it back until he was convinced it was absolutely ready. The Leppards, too, knew that this one had to be more than a killer. It had to be – to borrow a well-heeled Ted Nugent phrase – a 'major life-destroyer'! So the band swallowed their frustration at the continual re-takes, even though 'there're times when you feel like turning round to Mutt and just strangling him because he just won't accept what you're doing. He just pushes you and pushes you until, two weeks later, you get it right – to his ears! And you don't even know any more because you've played it so often! But when you do come out of it you can appreciate he *was* right and it *does* sound better. It's just a pain when you're actually doing it!'

Fortunately, no blows were struck at the producer but the recording of *Pyromania* did yield one casualty: Pete Willis.

For some time Pete had been growing apart from the rest of the band and it became obvious through the extensive touring the previous year that all was far from well with the guitarist. Pete seemed unable to cope with the constant pressures of being in a top-flight rock band and having to be on the go twenty-four hours a day. The continual touring, the incessant harassment from the well-meaning but often misguided fans, all the other little problems that crop up along the way, the minor discomforts and hassles that are part-and-parcel of being in a band headed for stardom in the way Def Leppard undoubtedly were.

Pete had never been the most outgoing of the Leppards, preferring to leave the on-stage guitar heroics to his partner, Steve. He had even been known to walk off the stage during the set in order to play out of sight of the audience. And as Def Leppard grew bigger the attention and demands on him naturally increased accordingly. Did Pete find himself more and more adrift? Was he able to handle the pressure adequately? He also discovered he was sliding away from his long-time friends in the band itself. This would have been particularly difficult as, and it should not be forgotten, Pete had been at school with Rick Savage. At this difficult time Pete admits that he found himself drinking more and this in turn seemed only to serve to increase the problems and his sense of alienation from the rest of the band. From the outside, from the fans' point of view, seeing their heroes apparently living the high life and indulging in all manner of luxuries that exist only in dreams or on the movie screen, this feeling of alienation is often difficult to grasp. But it does exist and is a common problem with stars thrust into the limelight unprepared to cope. The dilemma was probably best examined in Roger Waters's album and movie for Pink Floyd, *The Wall*. Anyone who ever scoffed at the complaints of rock stars as they are cut off from normal life should take a look or listen to this work to understand just what was going through Pete Willis's mind at the time. He apparently found some comfort in alcohol and this, too, was a problem that would later come back to haunt Def Leppard.

Meanwhile, as the pressures of recording the new album built up through the spring of 1983, the working environment deteriorated further. It became obvious to everyone around him that Pete was not cut out for the rock 'n' roll superstar lifestyle with all its extraordinary attendant stresses and demands. Similarly his attitude towards the work on the new album and the group in general was becoming very counter-productive and, worst of all, they could see he was destroying himself.

Try as they might to persuade the guitarist to pull himself together their advice simply fell on deaf ears and Pete seemed locked into a plummeting spiral that threatened to drag the band down with him. By the beginning of July there was no choice but to ask him to leave, a painful decision but one that had to be taken to ensure the continuing success of the band, the band the five of them had struggled so hard and for so long to turn into the success it had now become.

The split was amicable enough and with no hard feelings, threats of lawsuits or empty pockets on either side. Pete returned to his home in Sheffield where, for some time, there was talk of him getting a new band together and, perhaps, one day challenging the might of what he had left behind. But this never came to pass. Pete seems largely to have resumed the quiet life from which he had been snatched to grasp his allotted fifteen minutes fame. He did set up his own recording studio in Sheffield and was involved in a band called Gogmagog, organized by broadcaster and entrepreneur Jonathan King. This band was moulded from a variety of 'New Wave Of British Heavy Metal' acts with former Iron Maiden vocalist Paul Di'Anno and drummer Clive Burr, former (and indeed later) Whitesnake bassist Neil Murray, and ex-Whitespirit and Gillan guitarist Janick Gers alongside Pete. They produced one single in 1985 which failed to set the world alight. Pete later put out an album through Polygram with a band called Roadhouse with much the same result. Given the way the Def Leppard story turned out in later years, this was perhaps the kindest thing which could have happened. Fame is a grim and unforgiving beast sometimes best left alone.

Whatever, Pete's contribution to Def Leppard's success, on the composing if not the performing side at least, cannot be underestimated. He had even written many of the songs that ended up on *Pyromania* and had recorded all the guitar backing tracks prior to his departure from the band. The album in itself stands as a fitting tribute to his work with the band. But for both parties the split was a very necessary move: for Def Leppard because they were at a very crucial stage in their career where they needed to be rock steady amongst themselves if they were to pass the upcoming tests of their strength and stamina successfully; and for Pete himself because it was obvious he was no longer happy being a part of the band and his health would ultimately have begun to suffer severely. The best thing, then, was to part company before any irreparable harm could be done on either side. Sadly, this was not a lesson Def Leppard were to learn sufficiently well.

So Pete Willis left Def Leppard, a band and a dream that had consumed five years of his life. It might be romantic to view Pete as another in a long list of rock 'n' roll casualties but in reality it merely served to prove once again that in the music business the only prevailing law is that of the jungle and only the strongest survive.

Pete found himself in a band suddenly snatched from the backwaters of Sheffield and placed on a world stage. Def Leppard's rise to superstardom was nothing short of meteoric but sadly Pete apparently couldn't adjust to the weight of the new demands and pressures placed on his shoulders – such was the newly acquired success of the band. One of the grim realities about the much vaunted rock 'n' roll lifestyle is that, for some, it does epitomize life in the fast lane and that life at that speed creates casualties, inevitably.

So with Pete gone his former guitar partner, Steve, suddenly discovered he had to deal with ten tracks that all needed lead guitar recorded over the basic bed-tracks that Pete had already recorded. From shared responsibility Steve suddenly found himself solely responsible for all the guitar playing. More pressure, more strain. The answer, naturally, was to restore a workable balance to the band as soon as possible. Def Leppard had always been a twin-lead guitar band, that was the way they worked best and that was the way they wanted to continue. The problem then facing them was where were they going to find a replacement?

Having posed the question the answer became relatively

simple. Within a few days of Pete's departure Phil Collen stepped into his shoes as Def Leppard's second lead guitarist. It was really that simple.

Phil is slightly older than most of Def Leppard, being the same age as Joe. But his experience in terms of actual perform-ance is far greater. Def Leppard is Phil's third band. He previously played with Girl, considered the *chic* end of the 'New Wave Of British Heavy Metal' and themselves sometimes the object of much derision and abuse from both fans and press alike despite coming up with some excellent songs! He started his career proper with The Dumb Blondes, a London-based five-piece outfit that, again, had leanings toward Glam Rock although they owed more to punk than Girl ever did.

With Girl, another twin-guitar band, Phil had toured Japan very successfully, supporting UFO. There the glam image of the band fronted by former actor Phil Lewis – who caught the headlines while in Girl for being a beau of actress Britt Ekland, and later found more lasting success with LA Guns – was entirely suited to the Japanese market. So Phil Collen became a guitar hero in Japan before anyone there had ever heard of Def Leppard! He also recorded two albums with Girl on Jet Records, *Sheer Greed* and *Wasted Youth*, contributing to some of the composition, so he was no stranger to a recording studio. But the real ace in Phil's deck – and also precisely what Def Leppard had lacked with Pete – was that he was so commanding visually. He was a 'born poser' and on stage he pulled out all the stops. He was just the kind of frenetic, exciting performer that the Leppards needed in their ranks.

But, of course, Def Leppard knew that much about Phil already since they had performed together on the same stage. Some months before Def Leppard had joined forces with both Phils from Girl, Collen and Lewis, for a few 'star jam' gigs under the name of 'Def Girl'. These jams were largely staged just for laughs, most notably at London's Fulham Greyhound, a venue much beloved of up-and-coming bands, rather on a par with the Marquee Club. The shows gave the participants a chance to run through a medley of old rock 'n' roll standards for their own enjoyment, as well as that of any punters fortunate to be in the audience. So at the time of Pete's departure from the ranks, the band were already well aware of Phil's prowess as a lead guitarist.

It took no time at all for the Leppards to invite the guitarist along for what was supposed to be an audition but was in actual fact more of an excuse for Phil to play the guitar hero. It took still less time for Phil to accept their offer of permanent employment and the chance to alter his status for ever – at the time he was driving a beat-up Ford Cortina, before long he would be behind the wheel of a Porsche! Officially he was still a member of Girl but that band's activities had all but ceased. They had been dropped by Jet for the second time, they had no management and no real prospect of negotiating another recording deal. The band continued for a few months after Phil split, replacing him in order to honour a tour schedule in Japan, but packed up altogether just a few months later. Phil had jumped ship just in time not only for his own benefit but also for that of the outfit he teamed up with, Def Leppard.

His arrival was the equivalent of a shot of adrenalin in the arm of a Def Leppard still somewhat shaken by their deteriorating relationship with Pete Willis. Phil's arrival also coincided with their *big* break in the States where the visual impact of a rock band is even more important than it is in Britain. And Phil's brash, flamboyant style complemented them perfectly. And coming straight from another two-guitar band meant he slipped into the Leppard format easily enough. He was just what the doctor ordered, in fact, to counteract a slightly ailing Def Leppard.

Phil not only brought along his by now famous Ibanez Destroyer guitar – itself a present from his first trip to Japan with Girl – but also delivered up his not inconsiderable songwriting skills. These had never truly been brought to light with his output for Girl but they would become more and more evident on future Def Leppard projects. But for now what the band really needed was his guitar playing.

When Phil arrived and became an official band member at the beginning of July, ten tracks were virtually finished with the exception of the lead work, vocals and guitar, and the synthesizer embellishments which were to be contracted out later. Phil stepped in and immediately unleashed his Ibanez over five of the tracks, 'Photograph', 'Foolin'', 'Rock! Rock! (Till You Drop)', 'Rock Of Ages' and 'Stagefright', supplying some of the album's most dynamic lead work. Here and there he added some rhythm guitar and bolstered some of the guitar Steve had already tracked. The rest of the lead work on the album was all Steve's.

So Def Leppard had solved all their guitarist problems in one fell swoop and Phil Collen could now stand proudly alongside them as an equal member. But now all the problems concerning the album were quite as easily mastered. There were problems with the keyboard parts for, despite the fact that Sav later dabbled with keyboards on stage, none of the band were proficient enough behind a piano (or equivalent) to supply the requirements of the songs. Mutt Lange therefore brought in Tony Kaye – most notable for his work with Yes and for being part of David Bowie's 'Thin White Duke' tour in 1976 – to handle the keyboard passages. But somehow this didn't work out as planned and at the eleventh hour the mysterious 'Booker T. Boffin' was called in by Lange to restore the synthesizer work. Lange and 'Boffin' had worked together before on the Foreigner 4 album, 'Boffin' being a pseudonym for electro-pop whiz-kid Thomas Dolby who, understandably from his point of view, prefers to keep his forays into the world of Heavy Rock as low-key as possible.

But even when the album was eventually finished in November it still took a further two months for Lange to mix it down to a state the notoriously perfectionist producer considered 'perfect' enough to be heard by the rest of the world. But his lengthy hours behind the desk, coupled with the band's equally strenuous input and the public's long, long wait, proved ultimately worthwhile. Because *Pyromania* was as close to perfection as Lange had hoped it would be. Def Leppard finally had a *monster* hit album on their hands, so much so that even they, in their wildest dreams, could not conceivably have imagined it possible.

When *Pyromania* was finally released in February 1983 it rocketed straight into a sales stratosphere and never looked back. Within two weeks it had entered the *Billboard* Top 10 where it remained for an incredible six months and over the course of the year it was topped only by the phenomenal success of Michael Jackson's *Thriller*, an album that sold beyond all sane predictions and has since gone on to become the greatest-selling album of all time. Even Def Leppard couldn't stack up against that kind of opposition! But *Pyromania*'s achievement was spectacular none the less and went on to ship millions of copies worldwide, becoming one of Polygram's most successful non-soundtrack albums of all time. But *Pyromania* was more than a mega-platinum hit, it was a milestone, a total reaffirmation of belief in everything Def Leppard stood for or had ever striven to achieve. It was a classic!

Pyromania included ten tracks of blistering Hard Rock and, at the time, Joe claimed it was for its production 'the best produced album of all time'. This is an extravagant statement, certainly, but not one that is without support. But however great the production on the album, it is the music first and foremost that sets it apart from all the other releases that preceded it in this genre. And the music was undoubtedly the finest Def Leppard had yet offered up to public scrutiny.

From the opening chords of 'Rock! Rock! (Till You Drop)' it was clear that Def Leppard meant business. This track is a foot-stomping rifferama with some rip-roaring guitar courtesy of the new boy. Next up is the smash-hit single, the ode to Marilyn Monroe, 'Photograph', whose video gave *Pyromania* a big push through massive airplay on MTV. The song also features a 'rock 'n' roll clown' refrain lifted from the David Essex hit 'Stardust' of almost a decade before, itself the title song to a successful rock movie starring Essex himself. Joe wrote this piece as a tribute while actually watching the movie and, in consequence, the whole song had to be re-written in the studio to incorporate it.

Following this is another rock 'n' roll romp in 'Stagefright', succeeded by 'Too Late For Love' which opens with a more gentle, subtle approach before building into a powerful yet restrained rocker. This was one of several songs on the album that showed just how far Def Leppard had matured as song-writers and all the effort put in by the band as backing vocalists and by Joe's concentrated efforts on improving his own voice were displayed here to great effect. Next up was the sound of a helicopter spraying machine-gun fire at the opening to 'Die Hard The Hunter', a track based on a soldier's experience in war and easily Leppard's most grandiose performance to date – especially considering none of them had been anywhere near a war zone! – featuring some stunning guitar work from Steve.

This is followed by 'Foolin'', another hit single accompanied by an impressive video. This one incorporated a mysterious black-clad woman harpist and Joe bound to a mesh board while lasers fired across his face. The visuals were appealing but not half as appealing as the appearance of the band themselves. While most bands who were producing the same kind of material as Def Leppard – commercial Hard Rock – looked old and sometimes overweight, Leppard were young, lean, healthy and clean-cut. (Joe, in the aftermath of the Reading Festival, had shed his excess pounds.) The image they put across was of hard, aggressive youths who managed to retain that kind of boy-next-door charm. How much of this was actually *image* and how much merely an extension of their real-life personae, given some of their later troubles, is open to question. But the point was that it worked. They were rockers, that much was obvious, but they weren't beer-bellied, gross, and dirty, which was the popular, if misguided, public image of the Heavy Metal band; nor were they old and pensionable like so many other bands in the AOR (Adult/Album-Oriented Rock) field. Visually and musically Def Leppard were just what kids (in America in particular) were looking for. And on their TVs they found Def Leppard, and on their radios they heard them too.

'Foolin'' starts with a mellow, acoustic guitar passage from Steve before the main body of the song bursts through and Phil unfurls another solo. Next up is the anthemic, Judas Priest-like 'Rock Of Ages', yet another hit single and video, this one featuring the band playing inside a cave setting and Joe success-fully freeing a sword lodged in a stone in true Excalibur fashion. The song also features the only lyrical reference to the album's title, and is actually meant as something of a joke, sending up rock anthems in general and pointing out that the things shouldn't be taken too seriously. After all, the whole point of rock is that it is supposed to be *fun*!

'Comin' Under Fire' is another powerful rock number wherein Steve really lets rip. 'Action! Not Words!' follows hard on its heels and continues much along the same lines, this one incorporating some fine dual-guitar work. But Def Leppard save their most ambitious track till last, the epic 'Billy's Got A Gun', a truly awesome rock song with a performance to match. 'Billy's Got A Gun' and 'Die Hard The Hunter' are longer, more carefully constructed songs that proved Def Leppard capable of far greater heights than simple three-minute pop/Metal songs. The fact that they could record such material offered much for their future. With these two tracks alone Def Leppard moved into a higher league and raised the expectations amongst fans and critics alike. They were not to be disappointed.

Even the cover of *Pyromania* was stunning, depicting a skyscraper caught in the cross-hair of, presumably, a missile-launcher and a huge explosion of flame billowing from the building's side as a result of the pyromaniac behind that cross-hair!

The album was released to whole-hearted critical approval and praise was lavished upon it from every angle. The only voice of doubt raised was some disturbing noise about how much of a hand Mutt Lange had played in shaping it. After all, Lange's name appears on the writing credits to all ten of the album's tracks. Were Def Leppard simply becoming puppets dancing to his tune?

Sav explained Lange's invaluable contribution this way: 'The thing Mutt does for us, apart from giving us a technically good sound, is to help us a lot with arranging of the songs, and that's why we've given him the credits.

'We have a tendency when we write songs to just get *loads* of different riffs or choruses or vocal lines and we end up getting a bit lost in piecing them all together; whereas Mutt can listen to ten cassettes with probably ten different ideas on each cassette and say: "Yeah, that riff I heard thirty minutes ago will go pretty will with what I'm listening to now." He can really fit it all together whereas it'd take us *months* to try and sort it all out. That's one of the reasons he is so helpful and he does a lot of work that most producers probably wouldn't do.' It also explains why the band regard him so highly and consider him practically a sixth member of Def Leppard. But as far as the composition of Def Leppard songs is concerned, Sav added: 'Myself and Steve both write, Joe does *all* the lyrics, and now Phil's got a load of ideas to put down so I don't think we're going to be struggling for new material.'

Far from it and since Phil joined the band and began offering his ideas – after some initial wariness as to how the band would accept the 'new boy' butting in with his suggestions! – everyone proceeded to get very excited about the prospect of re-entering the studio to record the follow-up to *Pyromania*. But that was all in the future and, with the success of the album, they had no need to rush into anything now.

But with *Pyromania* in the stores at long last, Def Leppard could now set about promoting it the best and only way they knew how. After fourteen long months they were itching to get back on the road and show off their new guitarist, but most of all their new songs!

CHAPTER NINE

ROCK AROUND
THE CLOCK

The obvious thing for Def Leppard to have done at this stage would have been to pack their bags and set sail for the New World in search of further rock 'n' roll fame and glory. But no, Def Leppard still wanted Britain, they still wanted to break the big time in their home country. So after a brief two-week jaunt around Europe they toured through Britain in March 1983 giving their countrymen their first taste of granite-Hard Rock *Pyromania* fashion. And they were now beginning to be able to fill the concert hall venues bolstered by the hysterically enthusiastic response the music press lavished on the album. Def Leppard had now seen both faces of the press: the vicious attack force and the warm, comforting, and nurturing power. But despite this nurturing, *Pyromania*'s first single, 'Photograph', failed to make any real impression on the British charts.

The only real disappointment of the tour was the fact that they had to cancel one show at the Nottingham Rock City when Joe developed problems with his throat again. But this quickly cleared up and the band promised to return to Nottingham as soon as possible to honour their commitment to the fans there. Even so, the tour was not the stunning, sell-out success the band might have hoped for, but by now a certain sense of fatalism had crept into the Leppards' attitude toward Britain. Really, they now expected nothing from their home country, having been left out so long in the cold. But every little gesture of goodwill they did now receive was considered a great bonus. They might well have considered at the time the old biblical truism of a prophet being ignored in his own land. They might not have considered themselves prophets, nor were they being entirely ignored, but, when compared to their reception across the Atlantic, it must have seemed that way.

With another successful appearance at London's Hammersmith Odeon behind them on the tour and the dates finally wrapped up, they did finally set off for the United States where *Pyromania* really *was* burning up and the record beginning to shift in quite phenomenal quantities aided by some heavy radio and TV airplay. There was even talk in the papers and on the airwaves of a repeat of the much heralded 'British Invasion' of the mid-'60s spearheaded by The Beatles. No one was actually comparing Leppard with The Beatles musically but it can have done their egos no harm to be talked of in the same breath.

Def Leppard spent all spring, all summer, and part of the autumn blitzing the States ensuring that *everybody* knew exactly who Def Leppard were and what they were about! They toured everywhere, the length and breadth of the United States, even taking in Hawaii in the summer although they had little time for sunbathing. Once again they were living out of suitcases and seeing the sun only on days off and through tour coach windows. The 'Pyromania' tour was exhaustive and stretched over most of six months with the band awarding themselves only a brief ten-day break at the end of July. This was life in the fast lane for real.

During the first part of the tour they occupied the support slot to American rocker Billy Squier, who was enjoying some notable success from his 1982 album *Emotions In Motion*. By maintaining such a high profile Def Leppard continued to push the sales of *Pyromania* in an ever upward spiral as more and more punters came to realize that the Leppards looked as good as they sounded. The atmosphere at the shows became astounding with their audience veering away from the purely mainstream, predominantly male Heavy Rock crowd and more towards an across-the-board pop/rock following. Heavy Rock fans were standing side-by-side with screaming teenage girls – the former attracted by their hard-edged sound, the latter by their youthful good looks – as Def Leppard assumed the awesome mantle of being all things to all people. In the States such an occurrence may not seem that unusual but back in Britain there are few acts that ever manage to pull off such a diversity of fan appeal. But the Leppards managed it: *Pyromania* had proved them musically capable of producing the goods, and now the accompanying tour had established they were visually capable as well. 'Photograph', meanwhile, had become their biggest single-hit yet, entering the *Billboard* Top Ten.

Joe Elliott had also taken to sporting a Union Jack T-shirt as a patriotic gesture reminding their American audiences that, even if their home country was still, at best, lukewarm towards them, he and the rest of the band were proud to be British. This accoutrement, during the course of the tour, sparked a new fashion craze as the fans were left in no doubt as to the Leppards' nationality. Suddenly there were Union Jacks everywhere. They appeared in their thousands throughout the audience as well as on the streets. It was better, and certainly more eye-catching, than any logo they, or any PR consultant, could have dreamed up. Suddenly, if you displayed a Union Jack it meant you were a Def Leppard fan. It was possibly just as well for the band that you can't copyright a national flag. The charge to the band on their merchandising by the end of the tour might have made a severe dent in their profits. And the merchandising was shipping in truck-loads! But the Union Jacks kept on rolling and even Rick Allen got in on the act and took to his drum stool in Union Jack shorts!

As the Billy Squier tour came to a close the time seemed right for Def Leppard to move up into the big-time, the major-league status, and set out on their own, their first ever headline tour of the States. As their support act they initially took on Swiss Hard Rock band Krokus, whose album, *Headhunter*, was doing remarkably well.

The tour was taking the band in front of anything up to 20,000 people per night. One of the largest-capacity venues was at Alpine Valley, near Chicago, where 24,000 fans packed in to see the Leppards play; the smallest they were performing to still contained around 8,000. But friction between the two bands developed over a series of relatively minor differences, and Krokus eventually left to be replaced by stalwarts of British rock, Uriah Heep.

But that wasn't the only incident on tour. Joe dropped something of a clanger when he referred to the city of El Paso, Texas, as 'the place with all those greasy Mexicans' after he had been awarded the keys to the city. El Paso is just across the border from Mexico and has a large population of Mexican origin. The remark kicked up a furore of anti-Leppard feeling with the band's records being banned from the local radio and the League of United Latin American Citizens calling for a nationwide boycott! Joe promptly apologized, explaining he hadn't realized the resentment such a remark could cause. Leppard were restored to the airwaves and to further make amends Joe contributed $15,000 to five different charities involved in youth work in the El Monte area of California, which has a similarly large Mexican immigrant population. Joe was persuaded to fly in specially from Paris – the tour having wound up by this time – to express his apologies personally to the El Monte City Council. It was a classic case of 'if in doubt say nothing'. Or rather, in Joe's case, ignoring such sound advice and then having to pay the penalty. Still, there was no long-term damage done.

Despite these 'down' moments, there were plenty of 'up' ones on their headline trek. Not the least of these was when they played two sell-out concerts at the Los Angeles Forum, to a total of 32,000 people! For these prestigious gigs the band flew in their parents on an all-expenses paid trip to show off just how well their 'boys' were really doing. For the band this was undoubtedly the highlight of the tour and for their parents it was certainly an unforgettable experience, especially considering some of them had never been outside the UK before!

And then they closed the tour with a gig to end all gigs, performing in front of an incredible 55,000 fans at the Jack Murphy Stadium in San Diego, California. With this achievement they closed their tour firmly established in the Rock Superstar bracket and reaping all the rewards that entailed, including financially. Def Leppard were now forced to become tax exiles from their beloved Britain. It was a cruel irony that just as they finally found acceptance at home they could no longer afford to stay there. At the kind of earning level Def Leppard were thrust into, the British Treasury has always imposed punitive taxes irrespective of which political party is in power. So Def Leppard followed down a well-trodden path of rock stars fleeing from the taxman.

But a rather better benefit of their newly found superstar status came in their popular mass-appeal. For instance, Joe topped the 'Rock's Top Vocalist' poll conducted by *Hit Parader* magazine, another US rock publication, above more established singers such as Judas Priest's Rob Halford, Van Halen's David Lee Roth, and Robert Plant, the former Led Zeppelin singer who had embarked on a solo career. The band as a whole also scooped the same magazine's poll for the 'All-Time Heavy Metal Song' with *Pyromania*'s 'Rock Of Ages' pushing Led Zeppelin's perennial classic 'Stairway To Heaven' into second place. It seemed that Def Leppard were not only America's top-selling act in 1983, they were also its most popular . . . even if they were British!

Throughout October and November the Leppards toured through Europe, consolidating their growing popularity in the burgeoning Heavy Metal markets there, particularly in France and Germany. Also included in the itinerary were Sweden, Italy, Spain, and Belgium, taking in some thirty dates across the Continent along with an appearance at the Dortmund Rock Festival in Germany.

After a brief holiday over the Christmas period, Def Leppard set off for their first ever tour of the Far East. They played to ecstatic audiences in Japan, traditionally always a very positive market for Hard Rock bands, where their fame had preceded them. Japanese fans are very attuned to what is going on in other areas of the world in the rock market but the band were none the less truly astounded at the response afforded them in Japan. They continued on that wave of success through Australia and finally into Bangkok in Thailand.

But despite all this travel on their extended 'Pyromania' tour across four continents, surely the absolute pinnacle must have been their pre-Christmas return visit to the UK for three dates. They played the Birmingham Odeon – long considered a home-away-from-home for visiting Hard Rock bands – Nottingham Rock City – fulfilling their promise to make good on their cancelled date on the previous UK jaunt – and rounded off at the Hammersmith Odeon once again, in London. That night, at Hammersmith, they revelled in the riotous demands for an encore. Finally, Def Leppard had come home to a country now on the brink of throwing open its arms to them like returning prodigal sons. Def Leppard had pretty much conquered the world and now, it seemed, the British public was at last prepared to forgive any previous 'transgressions' and accept them as new Hard Rock heroes. Maybe, just maybe, there was a little voice whispering in each of the Leppards' ears, saying: 'Not before time!'

CHAPTER TEN

CRASH 'N' BURN

The 1983 festivities were rounded off with a slap-up party at the Chelsea Football Club ground in West London, attended by luminaries from the rock world including Billy Gibbons from ZZ Top – another band experiencing a renaissance after years of continual plugging away at the British market – that stamped the official seal of approval on their most successful year to date. The celebrations lasted into the small hours of the morning, when the five members of the troupe headed from their separate homes to spend a quiet Christmas with their families. All, that is, except Phil Collen. Phil was otherwise engaged in the purchase of a new house for himself in London and meanwhile sporting his new black Porsche and solid gold wristwatch as exhibits of his rise to rock superstardom. In the process, however, like the rest of the band, he had become a tax exile and could afford to spend only a limited number of days in the country and was thus forced off-shore over the Christmas period by the ever vigilant Inland Revenue. Def Leppard Central was no longer Sheffield but had been decamped to Dublin, Eire, where artists of all kinds are given extraordinarily generous tax breaks by the Irish government. So for the Leppards, given that they could get British newspapers, pick up British TV and radio signals, and were also only a forty-five-minute plane journey from London, Dublin seemed the ideal spot. It had many of the benefits of being at home without the decisive disadvantage of being clobbered for supertax on their earnings.

The new year ushered in a long-awaited and much needed session of R&R: Rest and Recuperation. The touring and recording schedules had been a gruelling test of their strength and stamina and now at last they could rest on their expansive laurels of victory. After all, they had earned it in all possible senses of the term.

So, for the first half of 1984, Def Leppard kept a low profile while they regrouped their energies. Perhaps their most daunting task still lay ahead of them: how do you follow a worldwide smash-hit album like *Pyromania*? The band resisted all temptation and pressure from within the record company to rush out a *Son of Pyromania* to cash in on its extraordinary success. They bided their time and waited till they had managed to stockpile enough new material confidently to approach a recording studio. To this end they moved *en masse* into a house in Dublin and began writing and demoing new songs.

But as the summer months wore on an old chestnut came up: what had become of Def Leppard? Similar noises of apprehension were expressed when it was announced that Mutt Lange – the man whose knob-twiddling skills had been a not inconsiderable factor in Leppard's emergence from relative obscurity to international renown – would not be available to produce the fourth album. So not only had Def Leppard pulled another apparent disappearing trick, but, more importantly, could they possibly hope to match the awesome power of *Pyromania* without the man many considered to be the power behind Def Leppard's throne?

In fact this wasn't entirely accurate, as Lange did turn up in Dublin to work on pre-production for the next album. But, given the lengthy and exhausting task of producing *Pyromania*, and that it was immediately followed by a similar tour of duty on The Cars' album, *Heartbeat City*, Lange was apprehensive about throwing himself back into the melting-pot before he'd awarded himself an extended break. But he agreed to work on the pre-production with the band. They had already laid down twenty-three backing tracks so work appeared to be progressing well. However, elsewhere things were not running so smoothly.

Manager Peter Mensch was already having trouble finding producers for two other acts on his roster: The Armoury Show, led by former Skids frontman and later British TV presenter Richard Jobson, and Armoured Saint, a Heavy Metal band from Los Angeles. Both these acts quietly melted away but at the time the additional headache of Mutt Lange's decision not to guide Leppard through the difficult process of topping *Pyromania* couldn't have come at a worse time for him.

The search for an alternative producer sparked off the all-too-familiar Def Leppard rumour mongers speculating as to who would be the person perhaps foolish enough to take up Lange's mantle. Initially two American producers were considered, Ted Templeman and Mike Stone, most notable for their work with, respectively, Van Halen and Journey. But both were rejected because, having defined their own sound, Def Leppard weren't anxious to graft someone else's 'hit sound' artificially on to their own music. So the search moved closer to home and Trevor Horn, who produced numerous hit songs for pop acts, Steve Lillywhite, who had made a big impact through his work with U2, and Genesis drummer and vocalist Phil Collins, who had co-produced his own solo albums, were all approached. Indeed, Collins was particularly interested but at the time he was too committed to a series of other activities to spare Leppard enough time.

Finally, in August, the speculation and name dropping was laid to rest when it was revealed that American Jim Steinman had come out on top of the pile of potential candidates. It was manager Cliff Burnstein who first threw Steinman's name into the melting-pot and, after some discussion, the demo tapes of the new album were dispatched to the producer in the States.

Steinman had been thrust to prominence in the rock world back in 1977 with the release of Meat Loaf's multi-million-seller album, *Bat Out of Hell*, which he wrote and arranged alongside producer Todd Rundgren. He comes from New York but spent his teen years in California and had become a student of the classical piano. But he forsook a career behind the piano keys performing to audiences clad in tuxedos and evening dress in favour of a rather more radical move: he formed a rock band with the unlikely moniker of The Clitoris That Thought It Was A Puppy, and all this before anyone had heard of punk rock. Returning to New York he had written a play called *Dream Engine* and then a musical entitled *More Than You Deserve*. A young Texan singer auditioning for this musical in 1973 was called Meat Loaf (real name Marvin Lee Aday); he had already released an album, and went on to perform in the cult movie version of *The Rocky Horror Picture Show* and sing vocals for Ted Nugent on his 1976 album *Free For All*.

After the musical Steinman and Meat Loaf toured with the National Lampoon Road Show – a kind of American Monty Python troupe – before Steinman wrote his next musical, *Never Land*, an update of *Peter Pan*, from which much of the material for *Bat Out of Hell* was gleaned. Then came that album and suddenly Steinman's name was everywhere. The album later overtook *The Sound of Music* as the longest-running album on the *Billboard* Top 200 chart and remains there to this day. But relations between the singer and the composer deteriorated and the follow-up album, *Dead Ringer*, despite a hit single, the duet with Cher, 'Dead Ringer for Love', failed to match up to its predecessor in sales terms. The two parted company amid lawsuits but were finally reunited in 1993 for *Bat Out of Hell II – Back to Hell* which raced to the Number One spot all over the world.

But in 1984 Steinman had moved his activities on to such acts as Billy Squier and his album *Signs of Life* and Barry Manilow – not a collaboration destined to gain him many brownie points in rock 'n' roll circles – as well as writing the smash hit 'Total Eclipse of The Heart' for Welsh singer Bonnie Tyler. Steinman's credits were diverse but his hit-making potential couldn't be faulted.

So, Steinman listened to the demos Def Leppard sent him and agreed to work with them. With that problem finally sorted out, along with Steinman and engineer Neil Dorfsman, Def Leppard, after a ten-day break, entered Wisseloord Studios, near Amsterdam in the Netherlands, to prepare their new album.

Mutt Lange's involvement in the project at this stage was restricted to offering advice from afar. If the stories are to be believed he was being sent demos of the new Leppard material which he then 'refined', adding his own comments before returning the tapes to the band. Certainly he was credited as co-writer on all the songs on the album that would eventually become *Hysteria*, as he was on *Pyromania*. But quite what Jim Steinman thought of this to-ing and fro-ing of tapes (if the story is correct) is not known. But as producer of the album and no mean songwriter himself it cannot have been exactly good for his ego or for whatever confidence between the band and himself that might have developed. But, in fairness to Lange, he had spent the time between his original withdrawal announcement and Leppard's entry to the studio convincing the band that they really didn't need him to hold their hands through this process, that they really could cope on their own. As it turned out this message would not finally get hammered home for some years.

But, as usual and following the pattern of the band's earlier trials and tribulations, the recording process ran into difficulties before too long. There are many different ways to record an album and many different roles for the producer to play in delivering that album to the listening public. After two albums under Lange's guidance Def Leppard had formed a fruitful working relationship with the man. In effect Lange had become a sixth member of the band. It is arguable that almost any intruder into this cosy atmosphere would have found trouble forming a new working relationship with Def Leppard but it soon became clear that Steinman's views on producing an album did not exactly match those of the band. Remember, Steinman was used to writing music and then having singers and musicians translate that composition on to record. But Steinman was always in control, it was him pulling the strings. Not so with Def Leppard.

One of the major bones of contention was over the guitar parts. Steinman, according to Phil, 'wanted us to play live. We wanted to overdub the way we'd done on *Pyromania*. And he [Steinman] would accept a lot of things that Mutt wouldn't.' And his guitar partner, Steve Clark, was no happier with the situation.

Joe, too, joined in the gathering chrous of disapproval for Steinman's method of working. 'He was a vibe-producer, not a producer of sounds. He wanted everything to have these big backing vocals.' In other words things were deteriorating rapidly. The situation and the general lack of communication between producer and band became so bad that the issue was reaching a critical mass.

In November Jim Steinman stopped working on the Def Leppard album. The basic tracks that had already been recorded were scrapped and the news suddenly broke to the outside world that the great parting of the ways had come, that the two parties had broken up due to 'incompatibility'. The sessions had appeared to be going well with Joe Elliott originally commenting that the sound was 'bigger, massive in fact' compared to what had gone before. But the split, when it came, threw the project back into months of delay while yet another producer was sought to take up the helm. Meanwhile, Neil Dorfsman had also left the project to begin work with Dire Straits on their *Brothers In Arms* album. So Def Leppard were left somewhat high 'n' dry, though they, doubtless, would not have much appreciated the quip.

An approach was made to Mike Shipley, who had also worked as an engineer on *Pyromania* and was, therefore, used to the way the band worked and the sound they were after. But Shipley was already working on the Loverboy album so had to be ruled out. Lange suggested they contact Nigel Green, with whom he'd worked on the *High 'n' Dry* album, as an assistant engineer. So the production job was passed on to Green, who now worked in a co-production status with the band themselves.

So a virtually new album was launched at Wisseloord with, this time, the guitar tracks being the first parts to be recorded. Overseeing this new session was Rick Savage, who just about set up camp in the control room. This time there could be no more mistakes. Too much time, energy and money had already been thrown away on *Hysteria* for any more mistakes to be allowed into the picture.

By the time the dust had settled around the studio with the disruptive comings and goings, Christmas had come around again and Def Leppard headed for home to escape the rigours of their increasingly frenetic recording commitments. They can have little realized as they packed their bags that this Christmas would be the last they would spend as quite the same unit. But their spirits were high and, they hoped, they had virtually finished their new album. But, after the unavailability of Mutt Lange, followed by the departure of Jim Steinman, fate, it seemed, had decided to deliver them a third blow, and this one the cruellest.

On New Year's Eve Rick Allen was driving his new American sports car, a Chevrolet Corvette Stingray, alongside his Dutch girlfriend Miriam Barendsen. Rick was on his way to see his parents at their home in Dronfield, Derbyshire, travelling south along the A57 coming from Sheffield. An Alpha Romeo, an up-market Italian sports car, overtook them and the two cars, as is commonly the case, became involved in game of cat-and-mouse, each attempting to better the other.

But while Rick was trying to overtake the Alpha he suddenly lost control and the car skidded off the road, somersaulted, and finally came to a rest upside-down having crashed into a stone wall dividing the roadway from a field. Rick was thrown clear from the wreck but had his left arm severed just below the shoulder by the seatbelt and the force of the impact of the collision. Miriam became trapped in the car, receiving head injuries that were thought, at first, to be serious but she was later released from hospital after a few days. The driver of the Alpha Romeo did not stop but disappeared into the distance.

For Rick, though, the situation was obviously much worse. Fortunately he was immediately attended by a nurse who happened to live near by. And a second nurse also chanced to be driving by and stopped to give further assistance. They managed to pack the severed arm in ice and thereby give some hope that it could be re-attached. He was rushed to the Royal Hallamshire hospital in Sheffield where an emergency operation was carried out by microvascular surgeon Mr Robert Page. This operation, an advanced, complicated and technically demanding one, was conducted within forty minutes of Rick's arrival at the hospital since time, in these circumstances, is always of the essence. This restitching of the severed limb involved an operation that lasted a full ten hours and then the anxious wait began to see if the re-attached arm would take. Despite being a part of the natural body and therefore not prone to attack by antibodies, as is the fate of many transplanted organs, there is no guarantee that a severed limb can be reconnected successfully, and even if it is that it will ever again possess the same powers it did before. Though heavily sedated as soon as he hit the hospital Rick was still conscious enough to have realized the extent of his injuries and their, apparently, catastrophic consequences. He screamed at Miriam: 'God, I'll never play the drums again!'

Sadly, it became obvious within a few days that the limb had not knitted in effectively and what was described as a 'significant infection' was reported to have set in around the join. The surgeons decided that the only course of action open to them was to amputate even though the hand and forearm were still in good condition. Despite this, Rick was otherwise in a healthy state and recovering fast from the shock of the crash and the other injuries he sustained.

The news came as a crushing blow to the band, Joe weeping on hearing of the tragedy. He had been at his London home watching the TV with his family around him when he received a telephone call informing him of the car crash and the drummer's condition. Sav, meanwhile, had been out shopping for a fancy dress costume to wear to the New Year's celebrations he intended to attend that night in Sheffield. Returning home he took a phone call. It was Peter Mensch relaying the news. Any plans for partying were immediately shelved. Later that afternoon Rick's parents called in on Sav and they all sat around in silence uncertain as to how or why such a tragedy had befallen them.

That evening Joe played a quiet game of snooker with his father; Steve and Phil, who had been reached by phone in their apartments in Paris, saw in the New Year in the company of bottles of alcohol; Sav sat in a daze at home in Sheffield; and Rick underwent the operation that would try to piece him back together.

The next day Sav visited Rick in hospital where things appeared to have gone well and he seemed to be recovering as well as could be expected. The following day Joe, too, visited the drummer *en route* to Holland. But the sight of his friend lying prone on a hospital bed was too much for him and he had to beat a retreat to the toilets where he could only cry and wonder what had gone wrong.

Joe, Sav, Steve, and Phil reconvened at Wisseloord on 3rd January 1985. They decided that the only thing to do at that point was to continue working on the album. They could sit and dwell on their fate and that of their friend but this would seem both defeatist and pointless. Far better to carry on with the album and try to put the events of the past few days out of their minds. So they set to work again since there was nothing they could do for Rick at the hospital, he was already receiving the best possible care, and they needed to be doing *something*.

Rick had already finished most of the backing tracks on the new album but clearly the entire future of Def Leppard as currently constituted was thrown into confusion. Within a couple of days of recommencing work on the album the band received the news that Rick's arm had become infected and had

had to be amputated. Rick's continued presence in the band was, therefore, necessarily in some doubt although the rest of the band and their management were sticking rigidly behind him. But the plain fact was in the music world one-armed drummers weren't so much few and far between as positively non-existent.

As Rick lay in his hospital bed he must have believed that his career had, like the Corvette, come crashing to an end.

CHAPTER ELEVEN

SCORPIO RISING

At the Royal Hallamshire hospital in Sheffield Rick Allen was slowly having his dosage of painkillers reduced and, at the same time, having to face the enormity of the tragedy that had overtaken him. He had lost his left arm and, he could only conclude, with it went the rest of his life as a drummer and member of Def Leppard. The conclusion was inescapable but it was not one he wanted to accept. As he was weaned off the drugs and his thinking became clearer and he could remember the events that had brought him to this position he could only see his life disappearing into obscurity.

In an attempt to ease the pain and anguish he was feeling at the time, his brother Robert moved into an adjacent room. He also did his best to lift the drummer's flagging spirits but, as far as Rick was concerned, he was a condemned man merely awaiting the passing of his sentence of death. And he knew how that sentence would be delivered: manager Peter Mensch would arrive at the door and tell him that, much as the rest of the band regretted the decision, he could no longer be a part of Def Leppard. After all, what other sensible decision was there to take? So Rick lay there in dread of that visit from Peter Mensch to bang the final nail into the coffin of his career as a rock 'n' roll drummer.

Finally, the fateful day arrived and Peter Mensch walked into the room. Rick lay on his bed, his head filled with fear, waiting for the death-knell to be struck. He waited in vain. Instead, Mensch passed on his best wishes and that of Rick's friends and colleagues in the band. And he told him to take all the time he needed to recover from his injuries. As far as everyone was concerned, Rick was still very much a member of Def Leppard. A weight was lifted from his shoulders. Somehow he had escaped.

With that burden removed he could rest easier and make a fuller recovery. But for a twenty-one-year-old used to the frenetic world of life in the fast lane, Rick found the biggest problem he had to face was boredom. Since he had lost his left arm and broken his right the best he could do was lie on his back and stare at the ceiling. The nurses had to prop him up in his bed and keep him moving to prevent bed sores and a general atrophying of his muscles. To enable Rick to do this himself they placed foam padding at the end of the bed that he could push against with his feet and raise himself into a sitting position.

Brother Robert, meanwhile, again to relieve the boredom, had brought in a stereo system so that Rick could listen to some music. At first Rick bridled at this, feeling, as he did, that he would never be able to play music again. And if he couldn't play it he sure as hell didn't want to listen to it!

But the tapes played on. And on. And since Rick was unable to get up and turn the stereo off he was forced to sit in his bed and be bombarded with this music. And before long Rick found himself, however involuntarily at first, tapping away on the foam pillows at his feet in time to the music. So the foam padding became drum pedals and Rick continued to beat out a tattoo to the rhythms emanating from the sound system.

When he was well enough to leave his bed and climb into a wheelchair the foot rests there, once again, served as makeshift drum pedals. Pretty soon Rick was causing general disruption in the hospital with his constant pounding in time to whatever music he could hear on his sound system or in his head. He was later to comment: 'Out of sheer boredom I used to lie there tapping my feet. And I started thinking: "Hang on a minute, this has possibilities!"'

Rick continued to make progress and pound away at whatever his feet happened to be resting on. Then, when Mutt Lange came to visit the drummer and noticed the incessant rhythmic tapping of Rick's feet, he happened to mention that, given the advances made in electronics, it might conceivably be possible to construct a drum kit whereby the sound could be triggered by pulses beaten out on the foot pedals. Admittedly, no such system actually existed in the world, as far as Lange knew, but it was quite feasible. And as far as Rick was concerned that was just the kind of encouragement he needed to hear. There was the remote possibility of some hope, some light at the end of his particular dark tunnel after all.

Psychologically, Rick was in good spirits once he'd fully come to terms with the loss of his arm and with it possibly his career. He hadn't realized at this stage that his arm had been briefly re-attached. This was possibly just as well at the time since, with the arm's failure to adhere properly, he could have become even more depressed when it had to be finally amputated. He wasn't aware, either, of the early visits from Rick Savage or Joe Elliott. Again, this was probably to the good since the one thing he didn't need was sympathy. What he needed was hope. So, despite the collective despair felt by the rest of the band, he didn't get sympathy and the visit from Lange had supplied the right injection of hope. When Phil Collen and Steve Clark came visiting from the Continent, Phil jokingly protested that the drummer was 'an inconsiderate bastard'! He had, after all, pretty much brought all Def Leppard operations to a temporary halt, at least for a couple of days. But it was the kind of thing Rick needed to hear, to be told to get better quickly and not hold the band up any longer than necessary. He later said: 'All that occupied me in hospital was what I was going to do when I got out. It was great to think positively. I had a tremendous urge to get out and start again.'

So tremendous was this urge, in fact, that Rick was dis-

One of the earliest known photos of Def Leppard. From little rocks to the giants of rock in just a few short years. (Dennis Lound, Sheffield Star)

Def Leppard Mk I, pre-fame, pre-fortune but still with Pete Willis (*far right*). Times change . . . (Rex Features)

Top: Early days and Rick Savage and Joe Elliott strike the right pose if for the wrong fashion statement. (Rex Features)

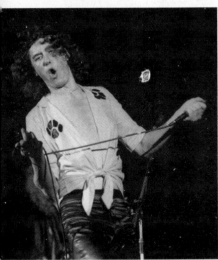

Above: Joe Elliott in archetypal Robert Plant mode. (Simon Fowler/London Features International)

Right: Rick Allen showing early 'Pyromaniac' tendencies. (London Features International)

Rather too much of a young Joe Elliott at Reading 1980. (Rex Features)

Joe Elliott on the US 'Pyromania' tour: No escape from glory. (Ebet Roberts/Redferns)

Phil Collen, new edition to the ranks of Def Leppard and a new chord to learn. (Neil Kitson/Redferns)

Rick Allen, post-accident, proves that nothing can keep a good man down. (Neil Kitson/Referns)

Above: Def Leppard Mk II, their attention not entirely riveted by the photographer. (London Features International)

Below left: Steve Clark, wild, carefree . . . but for how long? (Ebet Roberts/Redferns)

Below right: Joe Elliott and Phil Collen doing what Def Leppard do best – rocking out. (London Features International)

Above: Def Leppard setting fire to the world on the 'Pyromania' tour. (Patrick Quigly/Retna)

Left: Joe Elliott gives an indication of his musical tastes. (London Features International)

Below: Def Leppard grab a little time off in San Remo, Italy. (Rex Features)

Above: Joe Elliott and Bruce Dickinson swap singing tips at MTV Europe's launch party. (Phil Loftus/London Features International)

Right: Def Leppard, Sittin' on the Dock of the Bay. (Patrick Quigly/Retna)

Below: Def Leppard MK III, and Vivian Campbell (far right) joins the party. (Randy Bauer/Rex Features)

Above: Phil Collen shows new boy Vivian the ropes. (Paul Smith)

Left: Joe Elliott has to chose between recording that tricky vocal part or maybe a spot of football. Obviously a tough choice . . . (Martyn Strickland/London Features International)

Below: Glory days and glory nights, Def Leppard return home to Sheffield. (Paul Smith)

charged on 29th January 1985, less than a month after he had been admitted. The usual recovery period for such an accident, including a full measure of recuperation and physiotherapy, is six months. But Rick had a goal that needed to be reached: he had a career to resurrect.

But first he had to cover the basics, like learning to walk again. Even once he was out of the wheelchair this was not as easy as it sounds. A normal body is balanced, its weight evenly distributed over two legs with an arm each side of the torso to balance the body and allow easy movement. But with one arm gone Rick's sense of balance was upset and he found himself listing toward his now heavier right-hand side. All this had to be compensated for: he had to learn how to walk again. But this was a comparatively minor hurdle to be crossed. Far greater ones yet lay ahead.

While Rick began his slow journey back to full health in Sheffield, the band were trying to carry on without him, continuing to lay down tracks at Wisseloord. Def Leppard were almost completely blown out of the water by the enormity of Rick's accident. They had tried to carry on at what they knew best but somehow, while the will was there the application was not. They wanted to work but, understandably, their hearts weren't in it. They were with their friend hundreds of miles away. 'We were in [the studio] going round in circles trying to get things done, but all the time at the back of our minds were wondering how Rick was getting on,' remembered Joe.

Rick, in fact, was getting on fine. Before he left the Royal Hallamshire, he had been visited by a friend of the band from Sheffield named Peter Hartley. Hartley was well versed in all things electronic and had been responsible for building Sav's bass gear. Putting their heads together, Rick and Hartley worked on a prototype drum kit which would enable the drummer to participate once more as a full member of Def Leppard. Clearly, as far as Rick was concerned, while he desperately wanted to remain with the band he couldn't be a passenger so if he was to come back then he would have to be able to pull his weight, and to do that he was going to need a lot of help first.

So, before Rick had even left the hospital Hartley had constructed and then returned with the pedals that would be the basis of his new kit. This kit would eventually be updated and modified by a Californian whiz-kid called Arnt Anderson. And when Rick eventually began playing professionally again the synth-drum manufacturers Simmons would devise a new, revolutionary kit on which Rick would be able to perform to his old standard. The main difference from the normal electronic kits Simmons generally supplied would be the vast array of foot pedals Rick would require to enable his left foot to take the place of his left arm. Once Rick had obtained this kit his comeback would be all but complete.

But this return to the fold wasn't just a question of extraordinary technical achievements by some electronic geniuses. It is also a remarkable testimony to the courage of a man who must surely have seen his whole life disappearing before his eyes. This courage was demonstrated later, in 1989, when a BBC documentary on Def Leppard was broadcast. The programme charted the rise to fame of the band. Obviously a large segment of the film centred on Rick's accident, what is known in the trade as 'the human interest angle'. Rick was taken, with his full agreement, back to scene of the crash. As he walked through the field describing events of that fateful New Year's Eve he was suddenly overcome by emotion and broke down in tears. This was the first time he had been back to the site where, for a time, it seemed as if his entire life had come to a full stop. A member of the television crew rushed from behind the cameras to comfort him. It was clearly a traumatic moment.

Later, in 1992 Rick took part in one of a series of programmes entitled *Fighting Back*. Hosted by actress Lynn Redgrave, each programme centred on a person who had overcome a shattering experience. Rick appeared on screen to speak of his disability and quite surprised everyone by his demeanour, handling himself eloquently and with a fair share of humour.

The programme not only centred on the accident but also his recovery and re-establishment of everyday life. The rest of the band and his wife, Stacey – he had, by this time, married his childhood sweetheart – spoke of his determination to return to physical normality and showed clips of Rick dressing himself and cutting vegetables to hammer home the point.

Joe recalled his first hospital visit to the audience: 'I couldn't handle it, he just kept staring at me. I went into the bathroom and cried.' Sav paid tribute to the drummer's resilience by stating: 'The determination to succeed was all Rick Allen's.' The programme also pointedly showed Rick visiting patients who had also lost a limb. One guy in particular had lost an arm and had customized his attachment with tattoos. He spoke of the encouragement Rick had given him to return to health as the two sat and joked together. *Fighting Back* showed Rick doing precisely that and many people were forced to revise their attitudes to both him and rock stars in general as a result.

Rick was fit enough to return to the studio before the end of February. The sight of Rick walking through the doors of the studio brought a collective sigh of relief to the rest of the band. Just a few weeks before not only Rick's future seemed in doubt but also, obviously, that of the entire band. While they had insisted on carrying on no one was entirely sure that they would be able to and their lack of progress in Rick's absence must have added weight to that argument. But, at last, here he was back again.

'The day Rick came back to Holland was the day this band came back to life,' stated a delighted Joe. They had not even spoken about the possibility of Rick leaving the band, but obviously the thought must have lurked ominously at the back of their minds. Rick thought that he could conquer this otherwise crippling injury and the band were backing him every inch of the way.

As his colleagues put down the tracks in one studio, Rick would lock himself away and practice relentlessly with this new kit in another. He wanted to get things right before he faced the band and if he was going to make mistakes he didn't want the rest of Def Leppard to hear them. It had been his strength of character that had pushed him this far and his pride in getting things right was at stake. Everyone had put so much faith in his skill and he was intent on not letting them down. But there was still a fair amount of modification required on the kit not to mention a period of painstaking recuperation still necessary for Rick himself.

But as Peter Mensch had told Rick in hospital, they would give him time. A point Joe was willing to stress. 'Nothing gets done in a single day. It was obvious from Rick's brilliant attitude that it was only a matter of time. Then one day he came in and played the whole of [Led Zeppelin's] "When The Levee Breaks" perfectly. We knew he'd turned a big corner and we could start to breathe again.'

By the beginning of March, Def Leppard had recorded six tracks with Nigel Green, albeit only at the demo stage of their development. These tracks were titled 'Run Riot', 'Gods Of War', 'Women', 'Animal', 'Loves Bites', and 'Excitable'. 'Animal' featured three false endings which would later terrorize the DJs when they heard them, and 'Love Bites' was by now a totally different song from the original version that was demoed in Ireland.

In June the band uprooted themselves from Wisseloord and moved to Studio Des Dames in Paris, France, to continue putting down tracks for the next six weeks. The latest track that they had been working on was called 'Fractured Love' and while in Paris Joe added his vocals, whereas virtually all the guitar parts had already been completed.

There were jokes circulating around the music biz that Def Leppard's prospective fourth album had apparently disappeared like the *Marie Celeste*. Sav was told one such joke by someone who quipped that Def Leppard should call their new album *Halley's Comet* as it was likely to be as rare a sight.

But out in Paris it was hoped that the project could soon be mixed and, finally, offered up to the world. Fully aware of the ridicule being flung their way Leppard knew that this album had to be something special, and they felt that by working along the same lines that Lange encouraged they were getting the balance needed. Critics and jokes may come and go but quality remains for ever.

But the eternity the album appeared to be taking looked as if it was drawing to a close. The prospective release date now was the autumn and, following the time-honoured rock 'n' roll tradition, the Leppards began to turn their thoughts toward live performance. So Sav, Rick, Steve and Phil set themselves up in their own rehearsal room on the outskirts of Paris. Their singer, meanwhile, was still ensconced in the studio laying down vocal tracks.

As the four of them rehearsed for the first time since Rick's accident the possibility of Def Leppard utilizing two drummers was raised. To this end a friend of Rick's named Jeff Rich, who had been employed with British singer Judie Tzuke, was invited to come over and sit in with Rick and fill in the flourishes that Rick had yet to master. Jeff had joined Rick, while still in Wisseloord, for a few practice sessions before they hit Paris. Although Rick was grateful for the help, there was an air of tension especially on Rick's side created by his frustration at not being able to complete the rolls he had been able to dispatch so easily before. But before long, and again with much practising, Rick was back to his old standard and this rehearsal time gave him the chance to experiment with a few new fills. Just as Rick had almost had to learn how to walk again when he came out of hospital, now he was having to learn how to play drums again with one arm. And this time there could be no teacher as the technical problems involved had, quite simply, never been tackled before. Rick was a lone pioneer.

Def Leppard felt very pleased with the results of their rehearsal sessions and the progress Rick was making in re-assimilating himself into the band and they began to thread together a prospective live set. Everything seemed to be slipping into place and, with the album all but complete and the band pumping themselves up to hit the road they awaited the arrival of Mutt Lange in Paris to cast his professional eye – or rather, ear – over the tracks that had been completed in his absence. Since it was Lange who had been responsible for producing the bulk of their material to date then obviously his acceptance and approval for what they had laid down was very important to them. But Lange was not to be so charitable.

Lange listened to the tapes and he was not happy with the results. He dismissed their efforts almost entirely. Having freed himself from his other commitment Lange had agreed to come in and work on the tracks slated for radio play but when he heard the proposed record he concluded that they needed to start again from scratch. Not only had he stripped 'Animal' down to its core but also required the band to write new material to replace tracks such as 'Ring Of Fire'. In almost as little time as it took to express his view, Lange sentenced the band to a further two years of writing, demoing, and recording. Their plans to take their new songs out on the road were immediately shelved and the joke about Halley's Comet suddenly seemed to be rather closer to the truth than they had ever thought possible. The rehearsals, though useful for Rick, had otherwise proved fruitless and as far as the album was concerned it was almost a case of back to the drawing-board. As for going out on the road, well, while their muscles may have twitched they had to be held in check. Def Leppard had an awful lot more work to do before they could see the spotlights again.

What made this enforced retreat all the worse was that while the band were stationed in Dublin – where, once again, they'd retired to start the process over again – the largest rock concert ever staged took place. On 13th July 1985 the Bob Geldof-organized Live Aid extravaganza was played out before a TV audience running into billions. It was estimated that something like one in four people on the face of the planet saw this broadcast or, alternately, for the lucky few, were actually part of the live audience either at Wembley Stadium in London or at the JFK Stadium in Philadelphia. As a means to raise funds to help the starving millions in Ethiopia, Geldof had persuaded the largest stars in the world to perform live on either side of the Atlantic. Queen, David Bowie, U2, Bob Dylan aided by Rolling Stones Keith Richards and Ronnie Wood. The Who, and even a re-formed Led Zeppelin lent their services. In fact, just about anyone who was anyone in the field of rock rolled out for the event.

Geldof had actually telephoned Mensch to ascertain whether Def Leppard would be available, but owing to the situation with Rick at the time of the call it wasn't feasible for them to commit to it. All the Leppards could do was sit in front of their TV sets and kick their heels. They knew in their hearts that they had at least another eighteen months in the studio in front of them. They had been working to a formula without the main ingredient, Mutt Lange. But while they weren't able to lend their active support to the cause of Live Aid at least one light had appeared at the end of their tunnel. They had finally secured the hands-on services of Lange to oversee the project. Compared to what Bob Geldof had been up to this may have seemed fairly inconsequential but to Def Leppard it came as a great relief.

Still in tax exile, Leppard returned to Dublin and the Windmill Two Studio. It may have not been the ideal setting but the thought was that as long as it had a decent mixing facility then it would be good enough. The mental state of the band was dark. Sav even considered leaving at this time, but the thought didn't stay with him more than one bleak evening. With Joe and Sav having their own homes, Steve, Rick, and Phil rented a house in Dublin, until Phil's Porsche was stolen from outside the front door. At this stage the trio moved to a cottage in Donnybrook. They moved all the furniture out and proceeded to set up a rehearsal area in the front room. Rick, of course, was practising non-stop, which, although disrupting to normal sleep patterns, didn't worry his house-mates. As far as they were concerned it just showed that he was getting back to his old self.

The last thing Def Leppard wanted to do at this stage was

sit at home and quietly atrophy. So, to get themselves out and about, various members of the Leppard troupe would gate-crash gigs, wherever and whenever they could. Joe accepted an invitation to join Elton John on stage at Wembley. But before he could join in the encore he had to sit in a car backstage and learn the words to Marvin Gaye's 'Can I Get A Witness'. He managed to improvise his way through, though. Elsewhere, Phil turned up in more Heavy Metal surroundings to join Mötley Crüe in Paris to run through the Old Elvis Presley standard, 'Jailhouse Rock'.

In the summer of 1986, after seemingly endless months in the studio writing and rehearsing, Peter Mensch came up with a plan to get the band out before the public again. He booked them on to the 'Monsters of Rock' package which would begin at one of the most prestigious festivals in the Hard Rock calendar, the Castle Donington festival. Thereafter the 'Monsters of Rock' collective hopped from one festival site in Europe to the next. It was a simple way of displaying their wares to a wide and devotedly Hard Rock audience across the continent with the simple message: 'WE ARE STILL HERE!' To precede these appearances in front of such huge audiences the band would have to have some warm-up dates and these were set up through a short tour of small clubs in Ireland. Def Leppard were about to hit the road again.

Jeff Rich, although by now having signed up with Status Quo on a full-time basis, agreed to join Leppard on stage to supplement the drumming. Rehearsals got underway in Dublin without Jeff, who was already touring with Quo, and also without Joe, who was busy laying down some more vocals in the studio. Jeff turned up for four days of rehearsals and then Joe freed himself from the rigours of the studio to complete the final week of run-throughs. According to Sav, 'At least one member of the band had been in the studio working on something every day from Christmas '85 to the summer of '86.' Small wonder then that Joe was pleased to be leaving the confines of the studio behind for a while. According to him, 'It's very easy to get depressed when you're stuck inside the same four walls for three years – it was a bit like sitting in our own shit sometimes!'

On 5th August, the band set sail from Dublin to Cork, as the prospect of playing live once again sent the adrenalin rushing through their veins. Sav admitted later that he was more nervous for this show than he had ever been before. A few shots of brandy settled the nerves though and before they could even think too hard about it they were on and into 'Stagefright'. The thousand-capacity Connolly Hall was by no means bulging at the seams but that night was one of the most important the band had ever played, not least for Rick. 'It wasn't just doing it that was important for him,' said Sav. 'It was doing it so other people could see him doing it.'

The plan was that Rick would play the first two tracks alone and then Jeff Rich would join him on a second kit for the rest of the set. Despite a few hiccups the gig was a success and all concerned could finally breathe a little easier. They could still do it! Even though he never used to drink before going on stage, Rick, like a teenager on a first date, downed half a bottle of brandy prior to going on. 'The minute I got on stage I was straight! I was just so frightened,' he admitted.

That first show saw Rick making a few fundamental errors. His timing was a little off and as he concentrated fully on hitting the right pad at the right time, so his overall timing suffered. But these were teething troubles and were only to be expected and as the tour got into a stride so Rick relaxed and began to play to his full potential. He said later that 'within the space of those first few gigs in Ireland everything started coming together so quickly I think I surprised everybody, including myself'.

Galway was presented with the Leppard show the next night, but when they arrived in Limerick they were informed that only 200 of the 1400 tickets had been sold. In an effort to boost the audience the promotor dutifully trawled around the local pubs that evening actually giving the tickets away! If the press had got hold of this fact at the time they would have had a field day. 'Def Leppard Forced To Give Away Concert Tickets Shock!' the headlines might have taunted. But the Irish press is not as venal as the British and to the British press Ireland is a far-away country of which they know little unless it has to do with bombs or wayward clergymen. So the embarrassment went unnoticed.

In the event, though, it simply didn't matter to the band. They were just happy to be out in front of an audience, however small, playing. They had gone from the sold-out stadiums of America to giving tickets away hurriedly in the backwaters of Ireland. Def Leppard thought it immensely amusing. Besides, the band, whether by their own choice or by order of the management, weren't talking to the press. The music press's ears may have been pricked in anticipation of their return but they would have to wait until the Donington festival to discover for themselves just what the new songs sounded like or what opinions the band might like to divulge on the prospects for the soon-to-come album. Assuming, that was, that it really was coming soon. After all, how often did Halley's Comet come round anyway?

After a couple of days off, the next show was scheduled for a small town on the west coast called Ballybunion. Jeff Rich had used these days off to fly back to join Status Quo for three dates on the Continent. He promised to be back in time to take up the sticks again in time for the show. At 6 p.m., the soundcheck was due to take place but the drummer still hadn't reappeared. He had missed his connecting flight from Stockholm and would have to be taxied the hour and a half drive when he arrived back in Dublin at nine o'clock. The band waited at the venue, The Atlantic Hotel, biting their nails. By half-past eleven, Rich still hadn't arrived – his taxi had broken down. The band had to go on without him. Rick, for the first time since his accident, would be out there on his own, with no back-up. But the gig went fantastically, and when the Quo drummer turned up mid-set he could only stand by and watch as Rick proved himself worthy of being the lone drummer in the band once again.

The next gig was in Waterford, and Rich agreed to hang out

with them to see if Rick had any problems. But there were none. Rich, who had watched from the sound desk, went backstage after the show and met Rick with the words, 'Well, it looks like I'm out of a job, then?' It was the compliment that Rick had been craving. Although he realized the importance of having Jeff Rich alongside him to take the pressure off while he got used to playing live again, Rick needed the spur of doing the business alone. He had proved to himself that he was capable and now the rest of the band could settle in the knowledge that Def Leppard would certainly remain as a five-piece. The last of the shows, in Dublin on 13th August, merely cemented this thought in their minds. Besides, Rich had already departed due to further commitments with Status Quo. Now Leppard could concentrate on the big gigs, confident, ready, and raring to prove to the public back home that they still had what it takes. They were on the 'Monsters of Rock' bill and that's precisely what they intended to prove they were.

The Donington bill that day sported six bands. Opening festivities were Warlock, a German band led by pin-up Metal Queen Doro Pesch. Warlock had laid the foundations of a reasonable fan base in Britain, many young males drawn by the allure of Pesch. But it seemed as if their brand of Hard Rock failed to ignite a glimmer of response from those further back than the front rows. Looking good never did anyone any harm in the music biz but if you have little else to offer then trouble comes. Warlock later disappeared from the Heavy Metal circuit.

The decision to place the next band on the bill at all had angered many fans. This was because they weren't a real band at all. Bad News were a four-piece outfit, the creation of comedian Ade Edmondson. Edmondson, who is actually no mean guitarist and something of a Heavy Metal fan anyway, had written a thirty-minute one-off comedy programme called *Bad News* about a not very good, not very successful Heavy Metal band. It hit the screens around the same time as the similar spoof, *This Is Spinal Tap*. But since Spinal Tap were American and they had a movie to back them they scored far greater publicity. In fact, to many *Bad News* was far funnier than *Spinal Tap* and was far more vicious in its send-up of the whole Heavy Metal genre. But many people saw *Spinal Tap* as an outrageous presentation of the world of Hard Rock. In fact some argued it was deadly accurate and hardly a send-up at all. It was left to Ade Edmondson's *Bad News* to do that.

Edmondson both wrote the script and the music for the show as well as starring in it alongside Rik Mayall and Nigel Planer – who also appeared together in the hit British comedy show *The Young Ones* – and Peter Richardson. The four were leading lights in the 'alternative' comedy group The Comic Strip. But, for Heavy Metal fans, *Bad News* went too far. Many of them, who already felt victimized by the press, the TV, and the radio, didn't much care for their beloved music being laughed at in this fashion. Bad News went on to release an album and the Donington show formed the backdrop to a second TV programme. To the assembled Heavy Metal fandom this was sacrilege. Castle Donington was a beacon of light in an otherwise darkened year and to have it tarnished for the benefit of a TV programme was met with a barrage of taunts, abuse, and cans from the audience. For Bad News, though, it was better than their wildest dreams. If the original intention was to show Heavy Metal fans as a pack of rampaging animals then the Donington crowd played up to their appointed role like master technicians. In fact they just failed to see the joke which, admittedly second time around, was perhaps wearing a little thin. One of Heavy Metal's great strengths is the passionate devotion it inspires in its legions of followers. But when those followers can't take time out to laugh at themselves then things have gone a little off-beam somewhere. So Bad News's appearance at Donington was brief and to the point, just long enough to get the required film footage in the can and when the band urged the crowd to pelt them with bottles and offal the assembled mass was only too happy to oblige. Edmondson couldn't have scripted it better if he'd tried. So who got the last laugh after all?

Heavy Metal stalwarts Motorhead were next to take the stage, and like Leppard Britain hadn't been too kind to them since the early '80s. Motorhead's leader is bassist and vocalist Lemmy Kilmister, a rock icon who had been part of seminal '60s rockers Hawkwind throughout their halcyon days. After he'd been ejected from Hawkwind Lemmy formed Motorhead, a slang term for 'Speed Freak' – one of Lemmy's more pronounced vices – in the early days of punk. Motorhead got their first gigs on punk-package tours but before long they found themselves adopted by the Heavy Metal community, turned on by their fast, loud, and dirty guitar, bass, and drum mixture as well as their fraternization with the Hell's Angels, the perennial rock 'n' roll outlaws.

Given to such company, it is small wonder that Lemmy himself has a fairly fearsome reputation. He is not a man who suffers fools gladly nor one who much takes to being insulted. And, as far as Lemmy was concerned, the Donington audience pretty much insulted Motorhead. It wasn't that Motorhead were terrible but after Bad News had incited the crowd to throw all and sundry at them, some thought that it was a good idea to continue the operation against Motorhead. This did not do much to improve Lemmy's mood. Midway through their set Lemmy cut the performance dead when the deluge had reached epic proportions.

'I've been in this business too fucking long to have you cunts throwing things at me. If you're going to throw things, get it over and done with. Anybody who throws it have the guts to come up here so I can kick the shit out of you!' Similar to the classic Dee Snider rap at the Reading Festival some years earlier when he invited the whole crowd round to the back of the stage for a fight, Lemmy had dissipated the bottle throwers' egos. Lemmy's message would have won no prizes for tact and diplomacy but then these were never his strong points. But the matter got driven home and the bottle-throwing ceased.

Def Leppard had been subjected to the wrath of the festival public back at the 1980 Reading Festival. From backstage the view out front must have brought back painful memories. Nevertheless, either because everyone had unleashed their bottles already or due to Lemmy's vitriolic attack, or quite simply because they played superbly, nobody was throwing anything at Def Leppard this time round.

When Leppard hit the stage the atmosphere was one of curiosity. Would they play some new tracks? Was Rick actually playing? Were they worth their star status in America? The answers to these questions were satisfactorily answered by the band in the affirmative. Apart from the lack of introductions – and this due to the lack of time, they were not in a headline position here – Leppard stuck to the set played in Ireland. They unleashed a flurry of guitars and there they were cracking into 'Stagefright' in the late afternoon. Leppard just went out and rocked. The only sign of Americana glitz were Joe's red track suit bottoms, but even this was tempered with his T-shirt which featured the front page of the national newspaper 'The Sun' and its infamous '[British comedian] Freddie Starr ate my hamster' headline. Following 'Stagefright' came 'Rock! Rock! (Till You Drop)', 'Another Hit And Run' – 'About the fucked-up state of England' teased Joe at the beginning of the song – but it was during this number that Leppard truly found their best and even had the confidence to indulge in some audience participation. 'Too Late' was followed by the first of the new tracks, '(Don't Give Me) Love And Affection'. 'Photograph' was next – 'From total rejection to total infatuation!' as Joe put it – surely what Leppard were achieving at that very moment on British soil. This was followed by a brief guitar solo and then 'Let It Go' kept things boiling before the up-tempo new number 'Run Riot' was aired to interested applause. 'Rock Of Ages' segued into classic territory with The Who's 'My Generation' and Golden Earring's 'Radar Love' amongst others before Leppard left the stage, by now safe in the knowledge that encores had been ensured.

'Wasted' and Creedence Clearwater Revival's classic 'Travellin' Band' brought the proceedings to an ecstatic finale. Def

Leppard could not have wished for a more accomplished return to home territory. Not only had they come back in style but they had also conquered the apathetic amongst the audience. The show stealer, though, was a little detour from the set they'd determined on courtesy of their Irish excursion. Prompted by Phil, when Rick finished a drum break, Joe asked Donington to welcome the return of Rick Allen. The whole festival site stood as one in recognition of his hard-won battle and loudly cheered the drummer. Rick, seated behind his kit, was so overcome with the emotion of the moment and the ovation he received that he was moved to tears. The long, lonely hours practising had proved themselves invaluable after all.

Rick summed up his feelings a year later during an interview admitting that he was really nervous before the show and especially because he knew that certain people in the audience would assume he wasn't playing at all. But as soon as he heard the rapturous applause his emotions got the better of him.

Phil later spoke of his feelings about the Donington show: 'It was bloody amazing, it was like, "Fucking hell, they're givin' us an easy time!" which was brilliant. I think they could see that we were graftin' away, so I would put that down as a turning point.'

The co-headliners The Scorpions could barely cope with the surprisingly good reaction Leppard had achieved, coming on just before them. Ozzy Osbourne finished the day off in typically bombastic style with his over-dramatic effects but this day belonged to Def Leppard and primarily Rick Allen.

The tour then moved on to Europe. Leppard were obviously content in the knowledge that things had gone so well at Donington that they were looking forward to the next stop in Stockholm, Sweden. Before they headed off to Scandinavia, Joe shot back to the Wisseloord studio where he continued to record his vocal tracks. Stockholm passed off fairly unmemorably apart from the sight of Steve sliding inelegantly across the stage when he slipped on a wet patch. The next show, at the

Zeppelinfeld in Nuremberg, Germany, found Joe suffering from a sore throat and Sav feeling the effects of food poisoning.

Apart from the home turf of Donington, the most important gig of this mini-tour was to be held at the Maimarktgelände stadium in Mannheim, Germany. Def Leppard's record label, Polygram, turned out *en masse* to witness the band, a highbrow meet-and-greet session took place in the backstage area, and all was going according to plan. The weather had been good and the band were looking forward to proving themselves in front of both a huge audience and their patient record label. However, just as they took to the stage the sky suddenly darkened and the heavens opened. The deluge was so intense that even Rick, sitting near the back of the sage, was soon soaked. After waiting so long to get back in front of audiences Leppard continued their set even though, according to Joe, 'the guitars sounded like banjos'.

What had initially been pre-planned as a showcase had turned into an act of defiance. The Iron Maiden vocalist Bruce Dickinson felt for the boys so much he ran out on to the stage with an umbrella under which Joe could shelter. For the sheer hell of it Phil and Steve donned kilts for the encore, a move that reduced Joe to fits of laughter. It was a bright spot in an otherwise frustrating afternoon. When the album eventually saw the light of day, inside the sleeve notes was a picture of that day in Mannheim – the band on stage looking like drowned rats, the crowd shrouded under umbrellas – and a narrative by the band which aimed to sum up the previous four years. They felt that the Mannheim show mirrored their existence and summarized that outlook by stating that life in a rock band wasn't necessarily a party all of the time.

Unlike the Donington audience and despite all the heartache and tragedy that had befallen them, Def Leppard still retained their sense of humour and still managed not only to come out smiling but to come out on top.

CHAPTER TWELVE

HYSTERIA

After months locked away from public view in a studio, playing live might well have been exactly what Def Leppard needed to revitalize their energies. But when the 'Monsters of Rock' tour was completed they still had an album to make. The honeymoon was over and it was back to the grindstone in the autumn of 1986.

Rolling back into the studio the Leppards felt invigorated but all the while knowing that the next few months would prove vital if they were ever to get this album off the ground. Initially, things went well with a new song being written when Mutt Lange discovered Joe Elliott tinkering with a riff in the studio. Lange declared the hook that had been unearthed as: 'The best hook . . . heard in ten years'. Producer and singer set to work on it and the tune would emerge on the album under the title 'Pour Some Sugar On Me'. It was to prove one of the stand-out tracks on the album.

But then, almost as if Fate had decreed that it couldn't countenance Def Leppard activities running so smoothly, at the end of November Joe contracted mumps. In children this is not a particularly serious condition but for adults it is painful as well as being highly contagious. As a result he was forced to retire into quarantine for a couple of weeks. But it didn't end there, worse was to follow. The very day that Joe arrived back in Holland to continue work was the same day that proceedings were brought shuddering to a halt once again. Lange was on his daily drive to the studio when his car hit a patch of ice. He skidded straight into the path of an oncoming van resulting in a horrific smash. Rick Savage, who had been in a taxi heading towards the studio, was shocked to discover the wreckage of both vehicles. The police at the scene informed the bassist that both drivers had been taken to hospital, Mutt with serious leg injuries, but with the other driver having lost both his legs.

Later it transpired that this last piece of information was wrong, but it made Sav begin seriously to question whether all this was worth it, whether there wasn't some darker, higher force which really had it in for Def Leppard. For Rick Allen, though, it was worse still. Lange's car crash brought back all the memories of his own accident. But he knew where Lange would want him to be – in the studio hard at work. For the producer his diagnosis was better than had been expected when he was first admitted. His leg injuries were not critical and, despite the fact that they were deemed serious, he took his lead from Rick's experience and was back behind the console within three weeks.

Lange had promised that the recording would be completed by the end of January 1987. But then the career of Def Leppard had been filled with predictions unrealized and promises unmet. No one was holding their breath waiting for this one. But this time he was correct. Def Leppard had made no fewer than three attempts to record this album and twice the recordings were scrapped. They had well and truly been through the mill on this one. They had tried, and failed, to work with two other producers but, when push came to shove, Leppard were forced to concede that only Mutt Lange had the right degree of expertise and ability to get on with the band themselves to enable them to achieve the level of perfection that the band truly desired.

The final track to be completed was 'Armageddon It'; the scene was the Windmill Two Studio in Dublin. After the final touches had been put to the song there were no wild rock 'n' roll celebrations. The feeling as Joe and the producer sat in the studio that night was rather one of intense relief. At long last they had the fourth Def Leppard album in the can. For Def Leppard it was the end of a long and tortuous road. But Lange's job wasn't completed just yet. He still had to mix the thing.

Two months had been set aside for the mixes, and for the most part the Leppards were quite content to give Lange a free hand to execute these on his own. During February the band returned to Wisseloord to record some B-sides for the prospective singles. These were mainly numbers that had been discarded as album material, and the job was a task that was accomplished in a mere ten days, practically unprecedented in Def Leppard terms but achieved largely through the band playing 'live' in the studio. Included in these sessions were 'Ring of Fire', 'Tonight', 'Fractured Love', 'Tear It Down', and 'I Wanna Be Your Hero'. It was the complete antithesis of the album's recording. For the rest of the time the band set about preparing for the tour which was sure to follow the album's release, now scheduled for July.

Needless to say, the album didn't quite meet that schedule. In fact *Hysteria*, as the album had now been dubbed, was released on 3rd August, over four and a half years after *Pyromania* hit the racks. The pressure on the band had been immense, to say nothing of their personal difficulties prior to its release, but now all that was ancient history. In the cut-throat world of rock 'n' roll, especially considering the 'liberties' Leppard had afforded themselves in the making of *Hysteria*, they now had to prove they could still cut it in the only market that, to a record company, really matters: unit sales! And *Hysteria* would have to notch up considerable sales if their extensive time in the studio was to prove worthwhile.

Def Leppard had spent an awful long time in their various studios. Indeed, they reckoned, on completion, that someone from the group had been in the studio recording something every day since Christmas 1985. The monetary cost of *Hysteria* was phenomenal. When everything had been added in the final bill totalled well over £1,000,000 ($1,500,000). While many might wilt before such a figure it isn't actually too surprising considering that Wisseloord studios alone cost over £7,000 ($10,500) a week. Add to that the Paris sessions which racked up costs of £120 ($180) an hour! And that was just to record the material. Throw in the living expenses of the band and crew members and, before long, it isn't so much a bill as a telephone number. Sav recounted the cost and what it meant in terms of sales: 'We were told that we had to sell four million albums to cover the cost. Fortunately, we weren't told that until we'd finished. A lot of it was our personal money that we'd put in and, to be fair, the record company had also put in a lot.'

But there weren't only financial worries. There was also some concern that, given the extraordinary length of time it had taken Leppard to record *Hysteria*, they might have fallen from favour somewhat. Hard Rock fans are an incredibly devoted breed but would they still be there in enough quantities and feeling forgiving enough to enable Def Leppard to rack up the four million sales they needed just to break even? How far could any set of fans be pushed? The Leppards were about to find out.

This concern was not lost on Joe, although at the time he insisted that 'since Whitesnake are in the Top Five, Ozzy [Osbourne]'s just been in the Top Ten, so have Poison. Kids don't just buy one band's album. There's plenty of room for everyone – as long as they have something to offer.' He did concede later that: 'We felt really ill at ease between *Pyromania* and *Hysteria*. When *Slippery When Wet* did six million copies we felt that Bon Jovi had stolen our throne.' Understandably then, despite the success of the 'Monsters of Rock' mini-tour, Def Leppard approached the album's release with more than a little trepidation. When asked if he was concerned over the length of time between the albums Phil Collen answered: 'It gets beyond fear when you've been away for the length of time we have. We felt that *Hysteria* as a project was exactly what we wanted so we didn't worry about it. It was either going to be a hit or a miss.'

The answer to that philosophical poser would not be long in coming. Preceding the album was the trailer single, 'Animal', released in Britain on 20th July, backed with 'Tear It Down', and sporting a circus setting in the video. The single cracked into the charts with ease, sneaking up to the No. 6 spot despite its DJ-testing staggered ending. The album duly went to No. 2 when it was finally released to the baying public. Whatever their secret doubts and fears Def Leppard needn't have worried. With the release of *Hysteria* it looked as if the great British record-buying public had forgiven and forgotten whatever 'crimes' they might have committed before and were rewarded with a smash hit. They could all breathe easier now as it looked like they had emerged from their longest and darkest tunnel into the glorious light of success on their home ground, as far as they were concerned their ultimate goal.

Hysteria had originally gone under the working title of *Animal Instincts* and clocked in at a virtually unprecedented sixty-nine minutes featuring twelve tracks of some of the finest material Def Leppard had yet put a name to. Leppard had achieved an almost archetypally perfect marriage of down-and-out rockers, radio-friendly hooks, and drop-dead ballads. Coupled with the pristine production on which Lange prided himself, *Hysteria* had it all. It was as if the album could have served as the template from which all other radio-friendly Hard Rock albums should thenceforth be cut. No mean achievement for a bunch of guys from Sheffield, even with a grafted-on Londoner.

The album was met with a wealth of stunning reviews, many centring, perhaps only naturally, on their prolonged absence from the scene. Nevertheless, both the album and the subsequent rave reviews served to post notice to the hordes of bands who had come up in Leppard's wake that the band who were once the uncrowned kings of the 'New Wave Of British Heavy Metal' had gone rather more global by now and could now be ranked up alongside any of the 'big boys' in the field.

Hysteria's range, depth, and power spoke volumes but its message was still relatively simple. It said: Def Leppard are superstars!

In *Kerrang!*, internationally recognized as the closest thing in the Heavy Metal world to a Bible and now under the editorship of old-time Leppard champion Geoff Barton, writer Alison Joy culminated her gushing review by suggesting that *Hysteria* was the ground-breaking album of the decade.

With the album in the shops the media merry-go-round began in earnest for the band. Sandwiched in between these intense interview schedules the band found time to rehearse for their upcoming tour. After spending so much time in the studio the band were promising a mammoth trek to compensate for their extended absence. The band wanted to play everywhere there was an audience waiting to see them, and Joe wasn't making idle threats when he said: 'We want to come back looking, sounding, and playing like we're four times the band we were in 1983!'

Even in Britain, on the back of the No. 1 chart placing, there was an anticipation for the tour which had been confirmed for late August running into September. Even the difficult London audience had been moved to forsake its scepticism and scurry to the ticket office where a second night at the Hammersmith Odeon was quickly selling out. Phil also seemed perfectly happy to commit to an incessant tour: 'Oh, we can take it. Course we can. We've got it in our heads to do it . . . We pulled the album off, didn't we?'

As a prequel to the major road slog ahead Leppard played three warm-up shows in Holland before the album's release. Although massive in the States, *Pyromania* had sold perilously few copies in the Netherlands. Therefore the two dates they played at the Nooderligt in Tilburg were very low-key, whereas the last of this trio of dates was a free festival where Leppard would make an appearance in the late afternoon before a crowd in excess of 100,000. For these shows they had to borrow lighting and sound engineers from Thrash Metal band Metallica, who were also part of the Burnstein/Mensch management stable, Q Prime. As expected the turnout didn't fill the small thousand-capacity Nooderligt hall but Def Leppard gave it their all and premièred three songs from the album, 'Armageddon It', 'Pour Some Sugar On Me', and 'Women' as well as 'Love and Affection' which had first been aired a year previously on the 'Monsters' trek.

The tour proper began its serious business in Dublin on 27th August. From here the schedule would be to journey around the British Isles, ending up with two dates at London's Hammermith Odeon in late September. The support band on these dates was to be another act who had caught the eye of the Q Prime management. Hailing from the Californian capital of Sacramento, Tesla had been signed to Geffen Records on the strength of their stunning live shows. Their début album *Mechanical Resonance* had perfectly married their influences of classic British rock bands such as Thin Lizzy with the flash of Americana prevalent in such luminaries as Montrose, Aerosmith, or Van Halen. They had first played on British soil at the London Marquee Club where their twin guitar attack had impressed the assembled throng.

They were the perfect foil for Def Leppard. Indeed, on some dates they were so good that they were stealing the still-warming-up Leppards' thunder in a fashion not seen on British turf since 1979, when a young rock band called Van Halen finally put the nails into the Black Sabbath coffin, although, at the time of writing, many believe (save for maybe their devoted fans) they have still to do the decent thing and lie down and die. Sabbath's vocalist Ozzy Osbourne left soon after that tour, apparently deflated and disillusioned that somehow the world had overtaken the band he had given his all to. Tesla would make such an impression on both a personal and a professional level that they would stay with the 'Hysteria' tour for the duration. It's also a credit to the professionalism of the Leppards that they weren't afraid of taking a hot new act on the road with them as support. Many headline bands take to the road with what is known in the trade as a 'T-shirt Band' to pad out the bill. A 'T-shirt Band' is one who can be relied upon to create such a level of uninterest amongst the punters who turn up for the show that they leave the hall and congregate instead at the merchandise stands and buy T-shirts. Def Leppard, though, wanted a quality act on their bill.

But how could Tesla, an unknown act, be out-performing Def Leppard? Part of the problem lay with the on-stage mobility of Joe, or rather lack of it. While Tesla's vocalist Jeff Keith rampaged around the stage, the Leppard singer could hardly move. During one of the first dates of the tour, in Belfast, Joe had been overcome by a rush of adrenalin and had attempted one of his famed leaps from the drum riser. He landed awkwardly and subsequently trapped a nerve in his back. It left him in abject pain for the rest of the tour, despite the attentions of an osteopath who would try and coax Joe into full flight preshow. To make up for their frontman being relatively static the guitarists would attempt to compensate by jetting across the boards.

But whatever the singer's problems, compliments were flying in Rick's direction from all quarters; the biggest one anyone could pay was that they had forgotten that he was now thumping with just one stick. He had managed to overcome all the mental fears and physical handicaps that might have dogged him and proved that, given the chance, he could be as good as ever.

'Stagefright' and 'Rock! Rock! (Till You Drop)' still heralded the band's entrance though far more material from the latest album was integrated into the set. 'Gods of War' benefited from a suitably dramatic light show, 'Hysteria' also made it into the set, and even at this stage they were including the 'Animal' B-side 'Tear It Down' during the encores.

After Britain came the big one and the Leppards' latest assault on the American market. The United States had elevated the band to the higher echelons where they now resided and the band's hordes of fans there had been salivating at the prospect of having Leppard return for these latest live dates. And the band knew, as does everyone in the music business, that if a band is to become massive and, more importantly, stay massive, they have to break the States and keep it broken. The Beatles and the Rolling Stones had created the mould over twenty years before and every British band who became internationally successful ever since had followed their lead: crack the American market. The album had been released on the same day as the rest of the world but in the States, where Leppard had been feeling most vulnerable owing to their protracted absence, instead of 'Animal' being released as their first single, curiously enough a less commercial track, 'Women', had been issued.

'We took a massive gamble which is now paying off,' reflected Joe a year later. 'We put "Women", an album track, out as a single before the natural single "Animal". Rule One: don't lose your hardcore fans or you can end up with a 95 per cent female audience, who you know aren't going to be there next year unless you release another hit single.' Although 'Women' didn't gain any Top 40 exposure it was heavily rotated on FM and AOR stations, the traditional listening homes of rock fans. Despite the reluctance of the pop stations to support the single the rock stations were playing the album to death and, coupled with 'Women', *Hysteria* shipped out 750,000 copies and was selling between 60,000 and 100,000 copies a week. In the first eight weeks the album was already nearing the 2,000,000 mark, halfway toward the all-important break-even point.

For their return to the land of the Stars and Stripes, Def Leppard had to come up with a live scenario which was different in the extreme. They had to have something that would separate them from the masses. Spectacular light shows had all been done before by the likes of Pink Floyd, and the shock value connected to Hard Rock bands was old hat. American rockers Kiss had taken this option to its ultimate extent during the '70s, so there was no mileage there. Besides which, Def Leppard were hardly the stuff of the typical shock rock band. Other bands had already done pretty much all there was to be done in the field of on-stage implements. In an attempt to outdo everyone else Mötley Crüe had recently been exploding tons of pyrotechnics and in particular Crüe drummer Tommy Lee had devised a kit that would rise out over the audience and rotate as he executed his solo! Rick didn't much fancy the idea of trying to top that kind of extravagance. But the challenge went out from the Crüe: follow that! So Def Leppard were pretty much forced to do just that and took their lead from a completely unexpected source.

Manager Peter Mensch had put his Heavy Metal hat away for a night and taken himself off to a concert given by the legendary crooner, Frank Sinatra. Sinatra may hate rock 'n' roll with a vengeance but he is still the ultimate entertainer and there is nothing that anyone in the field of rock can teach him about putting on a show. What Sinatra doesn't know about the subject probably either hasn't been invented yet or simply isn't worth knowing anyway. There is a whole stack of wisdom stored away in the Frank Sinatra library that can be plundered by a sharp operator from the rock 'n' roll side of the fence.

Mensch saw immediately the answer to Leppard's problem of how to stage their American show as soon as Sinatra appeared. He was performing 'in the round'; in other words the stage was set up in the centre of the arena, surrounded on all sides by seating. So impressed with this concept was Mensch that he instantly commissioned a similar setup for Def Leppard. Leppard weren't the first band to play 'in the round' – indeed, ageing rockers Yes had pulled off the same trick a decade earlier, but a decade is a long time in rock 'n' roll and as far as most of the fans were concerned it was a lifetime – but they certainly succeeded in bringing the concept back into vogue. Indeed, 'trend-setter' Prince performed 'in the round' the very next year on his 'Lovesexy' world tour. One up for Def Leppard, or at least Frank Sinatra. But for Leppard this neat trick was just the difference they needed to make a lasting impact.

By having the stage in the middle of the huge arenas Leppard were now accustomed to playing they enjoyed the advantage of quadrupling the front rows. Not only that but they had also created an extra four thousand odd seats per show which would normally have been sealed off behind the stage. The fact that Leppard were selling these venues to within three thousand of the new capacity led many sceptics to believe that there was a shortfall when in reality Leppard were selling over a thousand extra tickets than would otherwise have been available.

Both the band and the fans relished the intimacy created in such big venues by the central stage. Initially some members of the band had aired doubts about the concept, but as soon as they'd actually sampled the 'in the round' stage these fears had been shelved.

The American tour continued to go from strength to strength. Increasingly Leppard would sell out more and more venues, despite the extra seats, and they quickly became the hottest draw on the concert circuit. Following 'Women', 'Animal' was released as a single and eventually it reached No. 19 on the *Billboard* charts. It took three months to get there, though, unlike the album. As Leppard rocked the audience by night *Hysteria* was selling heavily by day and on the back of 'Animal' it sold another million and a half copies. The added incentive of having 'Animal' in the charts, and thereby receiving both extensive radio play and MTV coverage, was also a bonus to the attendances. The 30 per cent or so of screaming girls which attended the Leppard gigs also boosted attendance, to ensure a sell-out. But while they ensured the sell out that would be pretty much as far as they got. By this stage Def Leppard were a multi-million-dollar operation and security is as tight on a touring band as on a diplomatic mission. No one gets backstage without a pass and to get a pass you practically need to sell your soul. Long gone are the days when touring bands would consume drink, drugs and groupies after a show. These days, while rock retains its mystique, the reality is rather more prosaic.

Meanwhile, back in the venues, the question on everybody's lips was: how did the band get to the middle of the arena without being detected? Were they heavily disguised? Were there hidden trap-doors? Did they have a system of dropping down ropes from the roof? The answer was that the roadies would push out large baskets apparently containing towels before the gig started. Unbeknownst to the massed audiences the band were hidden in these baskets. Joe would usually draw the short straw and have to share a basket with Steve Clark, a task which was made all the more difficult by Steve's claustro-phobia so Joe would have to spend the trip from the dressing-room to the stage calming him down. Once behind the curtain surrounding the stage the five would hop out and, shortly after, the show would start. But this was the only act of deception pulled by the band.

They were not averse to 'messing' with their audience's heads while out on the road. Rick would put on a jacket and stuff the left arm. Wearing a hat and shades he would then walk around the venue with, apparently, both hands tucked in the jacket pockets. When the fans saw this figure walking around with a big sign pinned to his back proclaiming 'I *am* Rick Allen' they would collapse in hysterics. What they thought they saw was some sad character desperately pretending he was part of a famous rock band. Cruelly they thought this highly amusing. But it was Rick himself who got the last laugh, collapsing into helpless fits of laughter when he returned to the safety of the dressing-room.

Rick was also the butt of the pay-for-your-lateness fine-system devised by the band. Basically, for every minute any band member was late getting on the tour bus they were fined one dollar which went into the pool for the end of the tour party. Rick was the main donator to this fund. He may have been a fine time-keeper on stage but off was another matter altogether.

Still off stage, all the frivolities of touring were evident but when it was time to be serious Leppard were the consummate professionals. Whereas Joe was on a semi-go-slow on alcohol to preserve his voice, Phil had given up the booze altogether after buying a £6,000 Rolex watch while drunk in Dublin while recording the album. The story goes that he awoke one morning unable to move his arm. Then he noticed that his wrist now sported an enormous new watch about which he had precisely no recollection. He then, allegedly, on finding the receipt, took the thing back to the jewellers and asked for his money back. The jeweller then, supposedly, refused to refund the money but agreed to buy the watch back for some trifling sum causing Phil to lose heavily on the escapade. 'I went through a hog-wild stage,' he admitted. 'Now things are different, different things excite me and give me pleasure.'

Hysteria's title track was next released as a single which quickly became the biggest seller thus far, pushing the album sales up to the four million mark. So, finally, Def Leppard could breathe easy again as the album moved from the red and into the black. Joe was obviously a happy man when the album surpassed its target. 'The *Hysteria* album is still in the [US] Top Ten and we're actually up on the thing!' he boasted proudly at the time. Def Leppard stayed out on the road in the States until the spring of 1988 when it was felt that maybe the country needed a break from them.

Pyromania had taken seven months to sell its first three million copies whereas *Hysteria* had achieved this feat in just five. By this time the band were also a household name in Europe. With this in mind the band returned to ply their trade in the concert halls across the Continent. The tour was scheduled to begin on 5th March in Stockholm, Sweden. From here it would wind its way through Norway, Denmark, Germany, France, Switzerland, Italy, the Netherlands, Belgium and Spain before heading across the Channel and playing dates at both Wembley Arena and Birmingham NEC, two of the largest indoor venues in the UK, ending with a night back in Ireland at the King's Hall in Belfast. The cost of bringing the whole 'in the round' stage set to Europe sadly made the idea of reproducing their American show unfeasible. Plus, of course, many of the European venues just weren't big enough to hold the 'in the round' setting. For example, the roof of Wembley Arena can support up to ten tons of equipment, but Def Leppard's set weighed thirty-two tons. The stage would therefore have had to be placed at the end of the arena and the fans would have had to be content with a king-size light show. The fans may have been disappointed by not getting the full show, but so were the band. As Phil commented: 'I think it's going to be a bit boring going back to regular stages. It don't half create a vibe having all those people around you.'

Originally, glam rockers Poison had been cited as support act, having achieved star status with their *Look What the Cat Dragged In* début in America, but having yet to tour Europe. It was felt that they would be an ideal lure to the younger punter, but the glamsters had to pull out for reasons well known to Leppard: they were locked in the studio finishing their follow-up album. Tesla carried on the job of support act once again in admirable style. Joe answered the critics of their earlier British tour and promised, 'That was at the start of the ['Hysteria'] tour, our first for four years. Now we're into this stage when we're starting to fly again and want to show people what we can do.'

Leppard were true to their word and weren't to be upstaged. The six months they had been on tour had trimmed them to a lean, mean, gigging machine. Joe was still having a few problems with his back, but nothing a massage before showtime couldn't fix. Leppard captivated the crowds and this time proved that they really were the band that until now the British public could only read about. Joe was overjoyed at the reception Leppard had garnered. 'We're experiencing the same buzz we had when we first broke America. Before this album we didn't mean shit in these places. Now all that's changed and it's great to be here and enjoying it.'

Following a brief sojourn in Japan, Leppard returned to America while back home rumours were emanating that there would be a new album from the band by the middle of 1989. More than likely this would be a collection of B-sides and outtakes and/or some live recordings. Nothing would be confirmed until the end of the tour which was currently snaking its way across North America. There was also some talk of a return to Europe for some 'in the round' shows or maybe a few festivals. For the time being, though, the band were happy to concentrate on the tour in hand. Whatever was to come in the future Joe was still singing the praises of Tesla: 'They have been very good. They remind me a lot of what we were like with our first LP, only they're one hundred times better . . .'

The triumph of the tour was soon usurped, though. Tragedy, it seemed, continued to dog the band. Before the show in Wisconsin in July, roadie and longtime friend Steve Cater suffered a brain haemorrhage while actually on the stage, dying later. The band carried on; by now it was the only way they knew how to deal with the traumas and tragedies life seemed to perpetually throw up. The tour just seemed to be getting longer and longer.

'Pour Some Sugar On Me' had been released as a single to accompany the tour and the whole organization had been sent into overdrive. Eventually, after eleven months of hard sell and hard slog around America's heartland, *Hysteria* had finally jumped to the very top of the charts. When questioned on the apparent cancellation of the proposed B-sides album a couple of years later in *Riff Raff* magazine, Joe answered: 'I'll tell you what put a stop to that. *Hysteria* put a stop to that. At that time it had sold five million albums worldwide so we were expecting it to tail off at the six-million mark like *Pyromania* did. At that time 'Pour Some Sugar' came out as a single in America and the album literally sold four million copies in three months. It went mental! It altered our whole schedule, so putting out our B-sides became a redundant idea.' So the album idea went on hold for the time being. A year later the video for 'Pour Some Sugar On Me' was voted the Number One video of all time by MTV viewers. It not only won but beat its nearest contender by two to one. The song has since gone on to become a favourite for striptease routines and has even been covered by the male strip troupe The Chippendales on an album they put out in the early '90s. In such ways has fame come to be measured.

As an example of the lengths some enterprising folk would go to in order to capture Def Leppard, Toledo DJ Jim Steel serves as a useful case in point. Disappointed that the overflowing Leppard schedule hadn't managed to incorporate Toledo, he challenged the band to a soccer match, live on air. If they lost they would have to play a gig in the city. Amazingly, Leppard took up the gauntlet thrown down and won the game 7–4. So no gig in Toledo, right? Wrong. In the weeks leading up to the game the radio station had collected 10,000 signatures on a petition. Leppard were so impressed by their persistence that Joe announced live on air that they would play after all. The entire ticket allocation sold out within the hour.

For some of these dates Leppard were playing outdoor amphitheatres therefore negating the centre stage set-up, but in Toronto they were forced to play at one end of the arena because the demand to see them was so great that they had to play a baseball stadium to accommodate them all. This, of course, had no roof from which to suspend the equipment! In Vancouver, on the last night of the Canadian tour, Bon Jovi, who were in the town recording, turned up for the encore of 'Travellin' Band'. The two bands, plus other party-goers, ended up at a club where they took over the stage and continued to jam till their hearts were content.

A new long-play video had also hit the racks. Entitled *Historia*, it was, as the name suggests, a run down of Leppard on celluloid, from their early beginnings and a dodgy BBC chart programme *Top of the Pops* appearance, to the glitz and polish of their latest work. 'There's ninety minutes of material on there, which makes it pretty good value for money,' enthused Joe. Also included was a video for 'Me and My Wine'; filmed in a house, it was inspired by the videos of the previously mentioned *Young Ones* TV series that the band had become addicted to on their tour bus. And as to that early *Top of the Pops* stint: 'That's the most embarrassing thing on there,' cringed Joe. 'We all laugh when we see it now, but at least it shows we've improved!'

Also improving was the chart performance of 'Pour Some Sugar On Me' and, in consequence, the album. *Hysteria* was fast overtaking the sales of its predecessor, *Pyromania*. As a result of the fanaticism Def Leppard became the first band ever to achieve back-to-back septuple-platinum (seven-million) selling records. As befits a band on the crest of a wave, they were being asked to carry on touring. Any plans to return to Europe were now out of the window, as was a visit to Australia, where 'Hysteria' had also gone to Number One. When they were asked to continue the American tour for a further few weeks the majority of the band were in favour of continuing to ride the wave. Not Joe, though. Despite the fact that promoters were virtually on their knees begging, he refused even though they were guaranteed sell outs. 'The rest of the guys were really bummed when I refused. Forty-eight hours later I said I'd do 'em, I was tired and my voice was knackered.'

Finally, after a mind-boggling two hundred and twenty-seven dates, the 'Hysteria' tour ground to a halt in Seattle's Memorial Arena in front of 15,000 fans. Along the way – in fact in Denver, Colorado, and Atlanta, Georgia – they'd even managed to squeeze in a film crew to record the 'in the round' show in all its glory. A video emerged the following year under the title *Live In The Round In Your Face*. At the very least it showed the fans back in Europe just what they were missing.

The band, meanwhile, retired to their homes safe in the knowledge that the painstaking recording process had been worth every retake. *Hysteria* was still selling and heading for the phenomenal total of fifteen million album sales. The album that could have broken them, physically and emotionally, had made them very rich young men indeed. 'Yes, we were,' admitted Sav later. 'Obviously you'd have to be stupid not to realize that if you're playing in front of 20,000 people every night, you're gonna make some money out of it.'

It looked to all as if the world was finally Def Leppard's

oyster. With each successive release Def Leppard had bettered themselves, exceeding even their own wildest expectations. As the tills continued to notch up *Hysteria* sales the inevitable questions began to be posed: How could they possibly top that?; and, perhaps more pertinently, How long would it be before a new Def Leppard product came out to attempt the task?

According to Def Leppard they had plans to release a new album after maybe a break of just eighteen months, comparatively short for them. Well, that was the plan. Plans, however, particularly where Def Leppard are concerned, have a notable tendency to become slightly unstuck.

CHAPTER THIRTEEN

TOO LATE BLUES

With a hit album, singles, and a massively successful – to say nothing of 'epic length' – tour under their belts, Def Leppard had been expected to slip quietly away and hibernate for a stretch. After all, hadn't they earnt it, not only in terms of sheer physical input but also in dollars? But there were one or two problems that prevented this. Firstly, hibernating for a 'stretch' in Def Leppard-speak could mean anything up to several years, and no one was anxious to do that. And secondly, there was that video to put together.

So *Live In The Round In Your Face* was spliced together from footage of two shows off the 'Hysteria' tour and unleashed on to the public. Well, that was fine, there was some new Def Leppard product out in the market place but, given the horrendous amount of time it had taken the band to come up with the last album, there was a general agreement on all sides that the next one couldn't be allowed to get diverted in the same way. This one needed to be rather more snappy, rather quicker out of the starting-blocks than *Hysteria*. For sure, the record company made the money they'd expended on the album back and then a whole truck-load on top, but . . .

And it was a big 'but'. The band had ridden their luck by taking so long with *Hysteria* and there was a feeling that if they were to take that length of time again then the fans who had so patiently awaited the band's apparent delays and prevarications

before delivery might not feel so inclined to repeat the performance in such unqualified numbers and may, indeed, not be
around to support the next album at all, or at least to the same
degree. Hard Rock fans may be traditionally loyal but there is a
limit to how far anyone's loyalty can be pushed. And perhaps,
ran the general consensus of opinion, maybe Def Leppard had
pushed it just about as far as it would go.

So studio time was duly booked, once more in Wisseloord
Studios, and the work on the follow-up began. But it didn't take
Def Leppard long to realize that they didn't need this, what they
needed was a break. Of the eight weeks of studio time that were
booked only six were used. A break was taken until the summer
of 1989. However, rumours were flying around back in Britain
that all was not well within the camp. The majority of these
whispers centred on Steve Clark and posed the question of
whether he was still part of the set up. In the past differing
Leppards always seemed to bear the brunt of these rumours at
differing times. But then Leppard, given their predilection for
disappearing from public scrutiny for long periods, are the
virtual unintentional authors of such rumours. When there is no
hard evidence to be had the press will always tend to offer
speculation in the place of that evidence. And then, as the press
well knows, why let the facts get in the way of a good story?

But this time the stories emanating from the camp had rather
more substance to them. This substance was given further
weight when the management issued a statement denying the
stories of Steve's imminent departure. Fatal move; the rumour
mills work in rock 'n' roll the same way they do with royalty or
politics: nothing gives a story greater credibility than an official
denial and the media vultures began to circle. As time passed
without any further development, it became apparent that Steve
would stay in the band, but more significantly that he had come
close to being asked to leave. There had obviously been some
serious words spoken and, presumably, an ultimatum given and
assurances of future good behaviour received. The problem
appeared to have been solved.

During the break, Joe Elliott came to the conclusion that too much time and money were being wasted waiting around for, and by using, expensive studios. He tackled the problem head-on by building a studio in his house on the outskirts of Dublin. Steve, too, had by this time set himself up in a house in Chelsea, a prosperous, well-to-do area of London much frequented by the likes of rock and film stars. Having lived out of suitcases for the past twelve years it was deemed a suitable time for him to put down some roots.

During the summer lay off Phil Collen had jetted over to Australia to produce a young Antipodean rock band named B. B. Steal. The album surfaced on the Phonogram label that autumn and garnered good reviews, but failed to sell in significant numbers. And, while that album hit the racks, Leppard's own finally began to take shape at Studio 150 in Amsterdam. But the spoke in the works was that they had to wait for Mutt Lange to become available again. So with Lange otherwise engaged elsewhere Leppard, taking Joe's advice on the unnecessary financial out-pourings, left Amsterdam and relocated to the singer's home studio.

The press, back at the rumour mill and with nothing really concrete to sling at Leppard, immediately began circulating stories of a major bust-up between Lange and the band. The outcome of this 'argument', went the story, was that Lange had been sacked from the project, the tapes had been scrapped, and the band had returned to Joe's studio in Ireland with their tails firmly between their legs. Finally in November the 'news' broke that Leppard had finally lost patience waiting for Lange. They had stopped work once again in order to accommodate him but to no avail.

The truth, however, was rather more prosaic. Lange had undertaken production duties on the next Bryan Adams album. Adams had, since the beginning of the decade, plied his guitar/ vocal rock style thoughout his native Canada and broken through into the mainstream with his *Cuts Like A Knife* album in 1983. However, he was to gain worldwide recognition for his *Reckless* album the following year. The singles 'Run To You', 'Heaven' and 'Somebody' were massive radio hits and secured Adams in the mould of a potential megastar. A duet with Tina Turner on this album, 'It's Only Love', gave Adams the opportunity to tour extensively outside the American continent and elevated him even further up the scale.

However, the follow-up to *Reckless*, *Into The Fire*, somewhat derailed this train of success and so Lange was drafted in to oversee production duties on his next attempt. But work, as was entirely customary on all Mutt Lange's projects, was continuing at a snail's pace. The album would eventually see the light of day under the title *Waking Up The Neighbors* and would include the theme song from the Kevin Costner smash-hit movie *Robin Hood, Prince of Thieves*, '(Everything I Do) I Do It For You'. This single, like the movie, would prove to be a hit around the world taking the album with it. So everyone might have had to wait, seemingly endlessly, for the latest Lange-produced album but it all proved worthwhile in the end.

Def Leppard remained on good terms with Lange but, bearing in mind their desire not to cause another massive delay, couldn't afford to wait for him to free himself from his other commitments. So they pressed ahead in Dublin instead. To aid them in production techniques Def Leppard called in Mike Shipley. This was no big turnabout for them as Shipley had assisted Lange in an engineering capacity for all the Leppard albums on which Lange had worked. Shipley, then, was equally well aware of how the band worked and what level of professionalism was required, as well as knowing the band members on a personal level.

While roping in Shipley was easy enough, getting together enough quality songs for an album proved more problematic. Before long the original idea of getting an album out within a year of the end of the 'Hysteria' tour had all but flown out the window. Certainly, songs had been written but factors largely beyond their control continued to dog their progress. Illness had hit the Leppards hard, various bugs had been picked up and passed on, and frustration was creeping in. But, despite all these distractions, the main problem still revolved around Steve.

Leppard, as always, were keeping very tight-lipped on the subject of their guitarist. Steve hadn't been seen in Ireland and everyone, naturally, wanted to know where he had disappeared to. Again the 'Is he in, is he out?' question was being bandied about, but unbeknownst to all those apart from a few close friends, Steve was in a desperate situation. Soon the world would know exactly how desperate.

On the morning of 8th January 1991, Steve Maynard Clark was found dead in the front room of his house in Chelsea by his girlfriend. Initial reports said that he died sometime in the early hours of the morning although a police statement ruled out any suspicious circumstances. Whereas an alcohol-related death seemed the most likely cause, many began to speculate on the use of drugs playing a major role. But this was a member of Def Leppard, and Def Leppard didn't indulge in those sorts of activities. Did they?

The shockwaves hit home hard across the world. Steamin' Steve had been a founding member of Def Leppard and had been the pivot in their twin-guitar sound. Had it not been for Clark, Leppard might not even have got started, as it was he who had threatened as far back as 1978, to leave unless the band broadened their horizons and got out of the rehearsal treadmill and on to some live stages. He had become the focal point for thousands of fans as he was the epitome of the rock star. His stage presence was second to none with his guitar slung way down low around his knees, his long blond hair flowing in the breeze created by him galloping, jumping and swirling before his audience. He pretty much epitomized exactly what the modern day Hard-Rock guitar hero was supposed to be.

He was thirty years old when he died. Steve's father had predicted that his son wouldn't make it to his thirtieth birthday. He outlived his father's prophecy by a mere six months. His last gig with the band had been that memorable final date of the 'Hysteria' tour before 15,000 fans. It was as fitting a farewell performance as anyone could have wished. Except that no one would have wished it. As with all musicians who are taken at a young age, he had far more to give.

The nature of Steve's self-destruction was the most boggling. Def Leppard were amongst the biggest rock bands in the world, and yet they seemed like decent lads whom the girls would be happy to take home to meet their mums. Their cover-up of the deteriorating Clark situation had been brilliantly executed. They kept their personal lives personal, private, and away from the media spotlight. Now one of their members had died through alcohol abuse. Their image of being the clean-cut boys next door was ripped to shreds. However, Joe saw things rather differently. He made his feelings on the subject of alcoholism quite plain: 'I think of it more as saying: "We're not sticking needles in our arms, or throwing TVs out of hotel windows."' Joe clearly saw them all on the same level and equated Steve's problem with the social conscience that deems drinking not to be specifically dangerous.

Rather than sit back and shun the inevitable media glare for a while, Def Leppard were quick to issue a statement on the matter. The band were obviously deeply upset by their friend's death. Joe's words captured their sense of loss: 'He was a really quiet, shy, humble, nice, gentle sort of bloke. It was a pleasure to know him and I'll miss him like a brother.' However upset the band were, there was no sense of shock contained in their statements. It was as though they had been expecting Steve's death. In interviews they were to give in the future it became clear exactly why Def Leppard had anticipated his almost predetermined self-destruction.

The important words in the statement were 'quiet and shy'. Steve had never been one to seek glory in the limelight, he never really fully got a handle on all the fame he found thrust upon him, and the saddest thing was that to comfort himself through all the pressures of stardom – and despite all appearances from the outside there are considerable pressures – he had turned to the bottle.

After the event, talk was much more forthright on his condition, which had up until his death been kept strictly under wraps. Rick Allen cited the fact that, whereas all other members of the band had other interests away from music, be it football, family, or whatever, Steve had only ever been interested in his guitar and making music. His only escape, apparently, was gained through abusing alcohol. And that escape proved, ultimately, all too permanent.

The original inquest, scheduled for 6th February, was deferred until three weeks later. On 27th February the Westminster Coroners' Court in London formally recorded its verdict on the cause of Steve Clark's death. The report stated that death occurred as a consequence of 'respiratory failure due to a compression of the brain stem, resulting from excess quantities of alcohol mixed with anti-depressants and painkillers'. Dr Iain West, head of Forensic Medicine at Guy's Hospital in London, said that the autopsy found that Steve's blood contained 250mgs of alcohol. In layman's terms this was the equivalent of being three times over the legal limit allowed in Britain for driving. Somewhat more significantly Dr West also found traces of morphine, Valium and painkillers present in his blood.

The events of his last night were also pieced together. He had become slightly bored sitting around in his flat and had gone out to a local pub where he had indulged in a heavy bout of drinking with a few of the locals. Rounds were quickly consumed and before long these beers were being chased down by spirits. Reports suggest that by the time Steve left the pub he was inebriated. However, once he'd returned home he continued drinking and, as his girlfriend had already gone to bed, he crashed out on the sofa in order not to wake her. He never woke up.

During the interviews subsequently lined up for the release of the *Adrenalize* album, the whole sorry tale of Steve Clark's alcohol addiction was made public. The sordid truth was told, partly as a message for those who were caught up in the same spiral of despair, but it seemed more that the band, who had been harbouring Steve's secret for so long, had to come clean about it. They had to get it off their chests, almost as if trying to exorcize the ghost.

Steve Clark had been an alcoholic for a long, long time. Try as the band had to help him, Steve would always slip back into his shell, taking his bottle with him for company. Stories that had been brushed aside, such as the rumours concerning Steve being fed Farley's Rusks – a savoury biscuit usually fed to babies – before shows just to soak up the beer and get him into a fit state to play, or about him attempting to smash his hands up in fits of nerves brought on by drink, were now being viewed as possessing a grain of truth.

It turned out that Steve had been an alcoholic for most of his musical career, but it began to surface as a serious cause for concern only in 1989 after the monster 'Hysteria' tour. The main problem stemmed from the days off. The tight schedules employed on days when the band were playing would appear to keep him on the straight and narrow. In other words, when he had a gig to perform, he had a goal. Having something to concentrate on kept him relatively sober. However, on the days off he would revert to type and drink himself into a stupor.

With Def Leppard always keeping personal matters as private as possible the truth about Steve Clark's addiction to alcohol was a revelation. It was not as if he hadn't tried to help himself, though. On numerous occasions he had booked into rehabilitation clinics, or attended Alcoholics Anonymous meetings. But all to no avail. It was plain for everyone around him to see that these visits were mere charades. The traditional psychology propounded by these groups is that to want to make yourself well you must begin by accepting that you have a problem. In Steve's eyes, though, he really had no problem to solve. And he was always there to put everyone else's mind at rest.

It was this sense of immortality that Steve believed he saw in himself that was wearing down his fellow band members. Too regularly they were called on to pick the guitarist up off the floor and put him to bed. The worse the situation became so the bigger the crutch the band became on which Steve would lean. At AA meetings in Dublin the form was that family members were required to stand in front of the group and tell how much pain and embarrassment the drunk was causing. Steve begged Joe not to tell his family of his predicament. Against his better judgement, but with the agreement of the Leppard management, Joe filled in for a family member. Every Wednesday for a month Joe would sit there telling Steve just what he'd done, physically to himself and emotionally to the band. Joe was convinced that when Steve would stand up in these meetings and declare that he was an alcoholic, he would have his fingers crossed behind his back as if attempting to negate the confession. Steve would attend these meetings but would afterwards pop into the pub on his way home. It was not a good sign.

By this time his nickname of 'Steamin'', instead of referring to his blistering guitar playing, had taken on a whole new meaning. As Joe had described to *Kerrang!* in an interview, by the law of averages, Steve Clark should not have died in his house in Chelsea. Instead he should have died in a gutter in Minneapolis. It was either a freak of nature or an iron constitution that had saved him that night.

While working in Dublin, the band received a call that Steve had been found comatose on a Minneapolis street. The prognosis was not good. In fact his chances of survival were deemed to be so slim that Joe, Rick Savage, Mutt Lange, and Cliff Burnstein immediately flew across the Atlantic to be at his bedside. When they arrived they found the guitarist in a psychiatric hospital. He might at that stage have been on the road to recovery but the facts of the incident pointed to a fortunate escape.

When Steve had been admitted to the hospital, he had registered an alcohol level in his blood of 0.59. When you consider that 0.30 would reduce any ordinary mortal to a coma, and that 0.41 was allegedly the amount that killed Led

Zeppelin's drummer John Bonham in 1980, the fact that Steve had not only survived but was recovering without any long-term physical damage was a modern-day miracle.

The doctor in charge of Steve's case asked each of his visitors to write a personal message, describing just what effect his actions had had on them, which they would read out to Steve in the morning. This was duly done and Steve broke down and cried. Quite simply, he just didn't realize all the pain he was causing. But as soon as they began to feel sympathy for him, Steve would turn the tables and be back on the booze. Later, while walking down a street, Phil, himself no stranger to heavy drinking, happened to utter a chance remark to Steve concerning the amount of alcohol in his blood that night. Steve responded with a huge grin as if to boast that he could handle his beer. It was the closest Joe came to hitting his long-time friend.

Phil and Steve had once been renowned for their drinking sessions, so much so that the couple had been dubbed 'The Terror Twins'. Phil, though, stopped his drinking and began to settle down to taking life a lot more seriously. Rick had been jolted into putting his life into much more serious perspective by the car accident. Rick had cut out his boozing when he married Stacey.

By September 1990, Steve's state had reached a crisis stage. He was turning up for rehearsals in such a state that he couldn't play. To a degree, this echoed the situation with Pete Willis before his departure from the band. With no immediate necessity to finish an album it was felt that Steve would be better served with an ultimatum. So Steve was given a 'conditional discharge' for six months at the end of which time he would be expected to return to the fold. Hopefully by this time he would have straightened his life out and returned to his duties in a capable state and be able to continue working on the next album. Obviously, had Steve returned to the band in the same condition as he was in in September, then the band would have had to conduct some 'crisis' meetings to decide whether there was a place for him in the band any longer. While he was away he was encouraged to write material at his own pace but without any demands emanating from the band.

So wary were Def Leppard of putting pressure on Steve that even phone calls were kept to a minimum. Steve's mental state by this stage was one of paranoia. It was known that if he felt that the band were checking up on him he would feel victimized and that the paranoia would only worsen. If that was the case then the band knew his first refuge would be the bottle.

As a means of keeping in touch with Steve, phone calls were made to friends to enquire after him. But it soon became apparent that he was still getting drunk. Ironically, Joe tried to phone Steve the day before he died. It's impossible to say what effect this call would have had on the guitarist but, unfortunately for all, Steve's answering-machine was the only connection Joe made. Whether Steve heard the call coming in and failed to answer, or simply chose to ignore it is, of course, open to speculation. But by the next morning he was dead.

In an interview in 1992 Joe made the startling confession that the band felt they had lost Steve a year before he died. So when the call from Cliff Burnstein reached the singer and relayed the news of his death, the effect was one of resignation rather than shock. They had all seen his demise coming and the band had, somewhat uncannily, readied themselves for it. It was one of those tragic cases of not 'if' Steve would die, but 'when'.

During those months leading up to his death, the remaining Leppards attempted to keep their lives on an even keel. Work on the album progressed earnestly, if slowly. Without the whole unit it was almost impossible to finalize anything. The band were in limbo, not knowing whether they would even have a fifth member come February. And if they did, would he be in any fit state to work? They were in the unenviable position of being caught between two stools and only time, it seemed, would provide any resolution.

From the very moment Steve died there was a resilience about the band. There was never any doubt, from their point of view at least, that Def Leppard would continue. The decision to play on had, in all honesty, been already taken in Steve's absence and with the songs all but finalized the decision was made all the more simple. Besides, Steve had lived and breathed the band and wouldn't want them to fold just because he was no longer around.

Immediately rumours started flying as to who would be brought in to fill the vacuum Steve had left. It was also clear, however, that Leppard weren't prepared to rush their decision. They might even continue as a recording four-piece, hiring an extra guitarist for road work. But if they were to draft in a fully paid up fifth member, the stipulations would be that he would have to be British, and would have to play exemplary guitar.

As soon as news of Steve's death became public knowledge, the ghouls had assembled. Calls were being made to Joe at his home; calls were being made to their record label; and calls were being received by anybody in the industry that might conceivably have a contact number for Def Leppard, all by those in the guitar fraternity eager to make a quick buck. Joe's response to all of the gold-diggers and their unseemly haste in attempting to cash in on the death of his friend was short, sharp, and to the point: 'Fuck off!'

With the shadow of Steve's death hanging over them, it was not to be until late February that the serious recording work began again. Between March and December that year the final 85 per cent of the recording was completed. As Joe was later to point out to those who were being in some way critical of the band for taking three years to issue an album: 'We actually spent two of those years arsing around and going through all kinds of shit.' Once again fate had played its hand and the dream of a relatively quick follow-up to *Hysteria* fell by the wayside.

While Steve had been experiencing the traumas of his worsening addiction, Def Leppard had been approached with a view to releasing one of their early tracks for inclusion on a compilation album being put together by Lars Ulrich, drummer with Metallica, another Q Prime band, and Geoff Barton, who by this time had been promoted from deputy editor of *Sounds* to the editorship of *Kerrang!*. This release was championing the impact of the 'New Wave Of British Heavy Metal' movement which had, indeed, produced a string of artists some of whom would, like Leppard, go on to achieve stardom.

But Def Leppard were not keen on attaching their name to such a project. Joe had always refuted the claims that Leppard were involved in that particular hype, citing his favourite bands as Mott The Hoople and David Bowie rather than the usual Hard Rock crop. Against their better judgement, and cajoled by Ulrich, Leppard relented and let him use their first anthem, 'Getcha Rocks Off', from their ground-breaking initial release. The album was issued in the late autumn of 1990. Once they'd heard the album, featuring cuts from the likes of Sweet Savage, Raven, Sledgehammer, and the Tygers of Pan Tang, Leppard realized they would have been vindicated if they had stuck to their guns. All in all it was a less than happy experience.

Although Lange was otherwise ensconced in the studio engaged in perfecting the Bryan Adams album, he still made himself available to Leppard, and had aided the band in arranging the songs that would eventually comprise the *Adrenalize* record. Indeed, Lange has writing credits on the bulk of the material that makes up *Adrenalize*.

Lange also offered advice to both band and producer to enable them to attain certain sounds or in correcting certain elements they weren't entirely happy about. Frequent calls were made to Lange to plunder his mind for ideas. To Bryan Adams's credit he took this in good spirit and didn't, as he so easily could have, put his foot down and insist that Lange concentrate fully on his own project. This process was actually helped by the fact that Adams's policy is mainly one of playing live and gauging a song's worth by playing it to an audience and noting their reaction. So the Canadian liked to get out of the studio as often as possible in order to find an audience to perform to. This gave Lange a few slack days when he could legitimately furnish Leppard with his expertise.

At one stage Lange almost procured one of Adams's songs for Def Leppard. The number in question was titled 'Touch The Hand'. This was a song that Adams didn't feel quite fitted in with the set he was preparing. So Lange sent a tape of the track over to Mike Shipley who duly played it to the band. Def Leppard loved the track and confirmed to Lange what a great song it was. But then Adams decided perhaps he'd been too hasty in dismissing it and hauled it back. Not unduly concerned over one track, Leppard concentrated on the ones they had already settled on.

Def Leppard were actually enjoying the relative freedom that Shipley allowed them in the studio. Perhaps they could breathe a little easier away from the 100 per cent perfection rigidly adhered to by Lange, and thereby allow more true emotion to flow on to the tapes. But the determination to produce their best ever effort on this album remained intact. The writing process had been a long and laborious one and a wealth of material had been discarded as being substandard. Indeed, this was material that many other bands would jump at the chance of getting their hands on. By Joe's own admission, Leppard aren't perfect and do write as much substandard stuff as anyone else. The difference comes in the fact that Leppard edit out the substandard material leaving only *la crème de la crème* to reach the public ears.

By March 1991 the recording had begun in earnest. There was no outward decision on recruiting another guitarist as yet, although speculation in the press was rife. The main contender for the vacancy was John Sykes. Sykes, it seemed, had all the right qualities for the job. First and foremost he was a native of the north of England, plus he also looked the part; his long blond hair and almost film star good looks had made him a popular pin-up among female Heavy Metal fans. He also had a very strong pedigree in the rock field.

Sykes had begun his career in a post-'New Wave Of British Heavy Metal' band from the north-east who had flirted, however briefly, with success, called the Tygers of Pan Tang. His stunning guitar work had caught the eye of Phil Lynott who duly installed Sykes as second player in the twin-guitar attack of Thin Lizzy, alongside Scott Gorham, around the *Thunder And Lightning* album and subsequent tour. Sykes's name was made. But when Thin Lizzy eventually collapsed Sykes continued to move onward and upward.

He relocated to the West Coast of America where he teamed up with vocalist David Coverdale. Coverdale's Whitesnake had been attempting to break the States for years and, with Sykes's help, the *Whitesnake 1987* album became one of the monster Hard Rock records of the '80s. However, the joy was short lived as the pair split acrimoniously before the tour. Coincidentally enough, a young man by the name of Vivian Campbell had replaced him initially for the video shoot for the first single, 'Still Of The Night', and as a result was invited to join the touring outfit. Sykes then followed his own path and formed a band called Blue Murder who had already released one fairly successful eponymous album by the time he was being linked with the Leppard post.

But Sykes wasn't the only guitarist whose name was tossed into the ring. Gerry Laffy, who had been a member of Phil's old outfit Girl, was also reckoned to be a distinct possibility. Since the early '80s Laffy, despite his obvious guitar-playing prowess, had fallen from grace. Whereas Phil had gone on to big things with Leppard, and Girl's vocalist Phil Lewis had relocated to Los Angeles to link up with the already established Hard Rock outfit L.A. Guns, Laffy had apparently sunk virtually without trace until he resurfaced late in the decade as a solo artist with his own band. But to do this he had to go back to playing around the club circuit.

In fact, in the intervening period Laffy had travelled to Australia and teamed up with renowned video director Russell Mulcahy who produced some of the videos that made Duran Duran famous on MTV, as mentioned previously. He also worked on some of the feature films Mulcahy went on to direct, such as the Highlander series. But as far as Leppard were concerned, in Laffy's favour was the fact that he had played with Phil already so the two could obviously mesh, he was British and that he knew his way around a fretboard.

But with speculation spreading like a minor plague, Def Leppard refused to add fuel to the fires by commenting. They simply referred all questions regarding the procurement of a guitarist to their Q Prime management team. When asked the all important query, 'Have Def Leppard got a new guitarist?' Q Prime answered monosyllabically: 'No.'

As work progressed it became apparent that Phil was undertaking all the guitar parts himself. On the face of it this would seem a massive job, especially considering the amount of overlaying and precision-playing required in Leppard's earlier recordings. And with *Hysteria* they had become not only the world's major rock band but had risen to a plateau where the company they kept in terms of record sales were the largest names in the business; they had joined the ranks of the *multi*-platinum selling acts. As a result of this high profile Def Leppard were producing a record that to some was not only on a higher par than their contemporaries such as Guns N' Roses and Metallica – they had, after all, been around a whole lot longer and therefore much more was expected of them – but as this record would be played on daytime radio they had to come up with a sound that would sit comfortably alongside the Janet and Michael Jacksons and Peter Gabriels of the mainstream pop world. No easy task.

Striving to achieve this feat meant many arduous hours in the studio. Phil re-recorded his parts three times. When he thought he'd found the right sound, he'd come up with another which he felt was better than the last. Although a mountainous task, Phil found the process a little easier due mainly to the fact that if he'd played one part, then he'd known exactly what was required when the next part was played. Instead of bouncing off a colleague, he would be bouncing off himself. There were obvious hiccups, one of which was overcome when Sav went in and played the acoustic parts on the track 'Tonight'. As the band record in mainly a singular fashion, instrument by instrument, once Phil's parts had been done he was free to return home to his wife, who had given birth to their first child, a son. In his absence Joe set about recording his vocals, a task that was to take a further three months.

In the past numerous accusations had been levelled at the Leppards as to whether it actually was them playing on the albums. This led on from the rumours of Lange's all-pervasive involvement in their product, that in fact the musicianship on the records was either his or that of session men employed by him. Well, that particular story finally got laid to rest with the recording of *Adrenalize*. Bearing the brunt of these sordid stories of musical ineptitude were Joe and, obviously due to his injury, Rick. The main bones of contention were that Joe fed his voice through a machine which would tune his vocals to pitch and that Rick allowed an unknown session man to play his parts. Joe countered the former by stating that everyone of any note in the industry now uses the voice-enhancing equipment. Joe was the first to admit that he didn't have the greatest voice in the world but that, ultimately, it was up to the individual fans to make up their minds whether they liked his voice or not. Indeed, he went as far as pronouncing: 'I'd cut my balls off to have half Paul Rodgers' voice.' Joe, being a big soccer fan, equated his position by drawing parallels between himself and less gifted footballers who have to work at their art to be able to achieve a distinction in their genre.

As to the drumming, Leppard let it be known that their technique of recording was to set up everything around a drum machine. Then the tracks were recorded around this with Rick laying his beats down in the final stages. So no anonymous drummers, unless you counted the machine and, once again, virtually everyone uses one of those in a studio now. With the advances in technology now open to them, Rick's drum kit had been updated so that the triggers were hitting almost instantaneously whereas before there had been a delay, albeit in milli-seconds. These improvements also meant Rick could update the sounds on his computer.

In the autumn of 1991, Bryan Adams released his long-awaited *Waking Up The Neighbors* album. Reviews of the fifteen-track record were very favourable, the only quibble amongst the critics being the overall sound. Many aired the opinion that it sounded too similar to a Def Leppard record. Bearing in mind the nature of Lange's technique and the fact that he had co-written all of the songs, this reception was hardly surprising. Once again Lange had woven his magic, and, on the back of the hit single, the album went to Number One across the world and propelled Adams into the major league alongside the likes of Leppard.

Meanwhile, back at the Leppard camp, the band were thoroughly enjoying their working relationship with Mike Ship-ley. Reportedly, he was slightly easier going than Lange, the consummate perfectionist, resulting in the Leppards being able to bend the rules somewhat. Before, any slight blemish in the recording process would have resulted in endless retakes to achieve the optimum performance. Whereas Shipley, taking a different approach, apparently let it go if he felt there was no detriment to the record.

Joe was full of praise for the knob twiddler and the sound they'd achieved for being a little less particular. 'The last album was a little smooth and clean, this one has more energy for being less perfect.' This was, he stressed, imperfections through choice and not through lack of ability. The imperfections made it a better record. The guitars, said Joe, were 'crunchier', the vocals more 'mannish'. But for the time being nothing but a great silence emerged from the studio. The world would have to wait till Def Leppard were prepared to unleash their latest effort.

Eventually, by December the album had been recorded. The anticipated eighteen-month gap between *Hysteria* and its succes-sor had now doubled and still the album wasn't released but it was at least in the can. Schedules were arranged, artwork commissioned, tracks came under the microscope with a view to single releases, and the whole ball-and-chain was readied to throw behind the album.

But simply recording an album isn't the end of the story. Now the thing had to be mixed. This is akin to a film being edited; the thing gets shot but, at that stage, all it is is a series of apparently disjointed strips of film. Only after the director and/or editor has been to work on it does it emerge as a completed movie, ready to be seen. Same with mixing. The recording is finished but now all the tapes have to be thrown into the melting-pot, correct levels found for the various instruments, maybe some extra sound effects added, whatever. And as if he hadn't done enough already, having co-produced and engineered the project, Mike Shipley readied himself to mix the thing as well. Def Leppard would have already been well aware of the workings of Murphy's Law – that anything that can go wrong will. They'd experienced it many times before and, even here, at this late stage, it came into operation again. Just as mixing got under way Shipley contracted hepatitis, a potentially lethal liver disorder. So everything went on hold. As a result release schedules went back and the promotional activity was put on ice. And the wait continued.

The absence of a second guitarist was still keeping the news pages of the rock tabloids busy, however. The original favourite, John Sykes, had, according to the media, as good as shelved his solo career and thrown his lot in with the Leppard cause. The basis of this story, apparently, was that Sykes had been spotted arriving at London's Heathrow Airport from Los Angeles. Phil had been seen to meet the guitarist at the airport and whisk him off to Dublin. Indeed, Sykes was seen around the vicinity of the studio.

So that finally answered that one. Sykes was the new guitarist. Except, of course, that he wasn't. He had merely turned up at the band's request in order to supply some backing vocals. Both Sykes and a session vocalist by the name of Dave Steale had been roped in to lend their singing talents and give the record more depth in the vocal department. So still no second guitarist.

With Shipley duly recovered from his illness the mixing took place and everything and everyone back at the record company was put on red alert awaiting the imminent arrival of the record. The title, *Adrenalize*, was derived from a passing remark by Phil. The band had collectively sat around trying to come up with a suitable title. But, as a result of Steve Clark's death, the suggestions emanating from the camp were on the darker side of black, none of which, of course, adequately reflected the content of the album. The album, despite all the attendant problems, was upbeat and uplifting. So they wanted a title to go with that feeling. When Phil suggested the word adrenalin the rest of the band jumped on the idea, bastardized the word and came up with *Adrenalize*. The name, they felt, would convey the sense of excitement and action the album contained and by adding the *ize* they would create something of a buzzword.

Before the release of the album, they would have put out a little taster to whet the appetites of those who had maybe forgotten that Leppard were still around. The first track, 'Let's Get Rocked', was the obvious choice. Its intro is a simple low-key query from Joe: 'Do ya wanna get rocked?' segueing into a classic, instantly recognizable Leppard hook.

Since the onset of MTV just releasing a single was no longer enough, a single without a video was heading precisely nowhere chartwise. Leppard had, years before, capitalized on this market and weren't about to turn their backs on it now. The Leppards, as became their stature in the market place, wanted a state of the art effort. Enter Steve Barron, a video director of the highest calibre, who had already conceived and directed two of the most impressive videos ever put to celluloid. The first of these was for A-Ha, a Scandinavian trio who had achieved plenty of airplay on the radio but who were struggling to gain the more widespread attention they so craved. Barron converted the band from pop wannabes to teen dreams in one fell swoop. The video for their single, 'Take On Me', comprised all the right elements.

The storyline centred on a young lady who dreamt of meeting her ideal man whom she had seen in a magazine. The video was stunning as Barron's effects found A-Ha's lead singer, Morten Harket, stepping out from the pages to make the girl's day.

The sheer excellence of this A-Ha video was then surpassed when Dire Straits asked Barron to lend his expertise on the lead single to be taken from their *Brothers In Arms* album. His work of computer graphics depicting two workers complaining about the easy life of rock stars in the video for 'Money For Nothing' captured the imagination of a public who were getting rather bored with the run-of-the-mill videos being churned out by MTV. Dire Straits, already a fabulously successful act through their album sales and live shows, before this, were suddenly catapulted into even greater success on the singles front. The video went on to win numerous awards and *Brothers In Arms* became the biggest-selling album in Britain, ever, and also spent four weeks at the top of the American charts.

None of this success was lost on Def Leppard. They knew they had to make an immediate impact on their return and if Barron could come up with the goods they would be laughing. The original concept of 'Let's Get Rocked' came from the American cartoon series 'The Simpsons', and in particular the lead character, the teenage tearaway Bart Simpson. Bart, through his elegant and eloquent use of slang and sheer rudeness, had become a cult figure in America. The original idea was to use Bart in the actual video, but this was felt a little restrictive. The video was to be part the teenage rebel, staying in bed, running down the street kicking over rubbish bins, and the like, intercut with the band performing the track. This was no ordinary performance, though: the band would be playing with no instruments – Barron would add these and the backgrounds later. It was a first for the animation technology used and would have a 'Heavy Metal *Fantasia*' feel. Joe reckoned the filming process made him feel like British actor Bob Hoskins during the incarnation of Roger Rabbit!

The single was released, with Def Leppard still a four piece, in March 1992. It immediately proved popular with the public. The video served every purpose the band had hoped for. So, with the release of *Adrenalize* just a week away, Def Leppard had every expectation that they would confound their doubters and once again prove themselves at the forefront in the continuing rock 'n' roll assault on the world.

With 'Let's Get Rocked' securing massive airplay in its first week, the anticipation for the album grew steadily. Then *Adrenalize* finally saw the light of day. The graphically striking cover featured an electrical storm going off in an eye. This was chosen, according to Joe, because 'The first thing you look at when you meet somebody, unless you're a pervert, is the eyes!' As expected the album was dedicated to Stephen Maynard Clark. A short requiem featured in the liner notes beginning with his influence on the band and then progressing to his struggle for survival. Only a paragraph long, the memorial ended simply saying that the band missed him. Steve, though not able to record any guitar parts for the record, left his mark by gaining writing credits for six of the songs.

Also gaining an unexpected credit was Mutt Lange, who had been credited as 'executive producer'. This was due to Lange co-writing the bulk of the material coupled with the fact that he made himself available to help the band in an advisory role throughout the recording. Rather than sweep his contribution under the carpet and take the plaudits themselves, Def Leppard, honourably enough, gave credit where it was due. Besides which there was no way the Leppards were going to deny the considerable influence the producer still had over both their songwriting and recording. To do so would have been to declare open season on themselves for any critic with an axe to grind in their direction.

All the gossip over Lange had, in essence, served only to deflect the spotlight away from Mike Shipley. Shipley seemingly tiptoed into the studio through the back door and carried off one of the hardest jobs in the business in exemplary fashion. While the record had retained the unmistakable Def Leppard stamp of authority, it also gave them a slightly rougher approach which had been previously smoothed over by Lange. Moreover, the record captured Leppard in a new light, as human, and therefore fallible, rather than mechanical, musicians. Joe praised the producer on the results of his collaboration with the band. 'It turned out to be as equally good as *Hysteria* but in a different way. I'm not knocking Mutt but the way that we did it gave it a little more of an edge.'

Most rock reviewers raved over the new product. Terms such as 'great', 'perfect', 'ultimate', 'staggering', and 'brilliant' were routinely lavished on the record. Outside the Hard Rock core other reviewers were rather less forthcoming with their praise but, however jaded and cynical the journalist, no one doubted its enormous sales potential.

Adrenalize's stand-out cut clocked up seven and a half minutes, lengthy for Leppard. 'White Lightning' was one of the most epic tunes the band had ever attempted. In fact it was only comparable to *Pyromania*'s 'Die Hard The Hunter' and 'Gods Of War' from *Hysteria*. Musically, Phil had come up with the tune during the 'Hysteria' tour. While going through the tapes during the summer break the recording resurfaced, but even though Joe was enthusiastic to develop the song Phil was undecided as to its merit. For his part he felt that the album would benefit from a better balance and preferred to include a couple of faster tracks to counter the ballads. But Joe felt the aura created by the song was similar to some of the fabled legends of rock, their musical mentors, and felt that this was Leppard's chance to equal Pink Floyd and Led Zeppelin with just one track.

Despite the grandeur of the song, the lyrics were to be the focal point. Joe delivered a compelling journey into the agonies of addiction. The understandable initial reaction was to reason that the song's storyline was an almost biographical tale that related directly to the final months of Steve's life. This impression was to be partly vindicated by Joe, but the song's inspirations went far deeper. 'While absolutely inspired by what happened to Steve, it's not actually about him,' reasoned Joe.

'We wanted to be totally open with the lyric, we wanted it to suit whatever position the individual is in.' The song could also apply to those legends of music who met an early end through addiction: Jimi Hendrix, Janis Joplin, and Bon Scott were all applicable names. Apart from show-business stars Joe also wanted to make it relevant to the guy on the street with a bad heroin habit or the neighbour with bad gambling debts. It was a song to encompass all the Achilles' heels of individuals. It was also important that the song didn't come across as the band talking down to the listener. 'We tried to write it without preaching. All we're doing is putting the information on a plate and whether you eat it or not is up to you. We spent a long time getting the lyric right in that sense,' explained Joe.

Apart from 'White Lightning', all the other tracks based themselves on the age-old 'boy-meets-girl', or 'boy-frustrated-at-not-meeting-girl' storylines. 'But not in a crass way, I don't believe,' the lyric writer pointed out. Leppard may have been guilty of crassness in the past but with *Adrenalize* had moved on to a new level. Even the vocalist admitted that the band had been guilty of 'being macho for all the wrong reasons. All that chest-beating frontman, wild-stallion-running-through-the-valley crap.' Def Leppard, it seemed, were growing up.

Adrenalize was criticized for its banal lyrical content. This immediately lined it up with virtually every other Hard Rock album produced over the previous twenty years. But a Def Leppard album is the wrong place to go looking for the secrets to Life, the Universe, and Everything. What is far more apparent on a Def Leppard album, lyrically at the very least, is an enormous sense of fun and jokes that may even have been aimed at just the same people who would then complain about the album's lack of 'political correctness' – the in-vogue term. Joe handled these detractors in his typically blunt Northern New Man style, especially on the topic of the much derided 'Make Love Like A Man'. 'It's a total piss-take. There's gonna be some chick hanging out around [British nuclear power plant] Sellafield in her dungarees who isn't gonna be too happy, but if they don't get it they ain't listening properly. All I've got to say to them is: "Get a sense of humour". If people miss out on the humour they're not listening right.'

Having been brought up on the glitz and showmanship of the Glam Rock sounds and images of the '70s, the vocalist failed to find a niche for politics in his lyrics. 'It's entertainment,' he protested. 'I'd rather listen to [Slade vocalist] Noddy Holder singing about nothing than do a duet with Sinead O'Connor. We've never been ones to make political statements, as we've always seen ourselves as the alternative to that.'

With that attitude in mind, 'Let's Get Rocked' set out the Leppard stall for *Adrenalize*. Much the same as 'Pour Some Sugar On Me' from *Hysteria*, it was also the last track to be written. Against the usual grain of Leppard recording, 'Let's Get Rocked' was written and recorded in just four days. For Def Leppard such speed was nothing short of a minor miracle.

While 'Let's Get Rocked' kicked things into gear, *Adrenalize* ended surprisingly with a track called 'Tear It Down'. The number had previously been available as the B-side to the 'Animal' single in 1987. The track had originally been recorded during the *Hysteria* sessions but as they spent only ninety minutes on the song it was deemed unworthy of inclusion on that particular album. But since the band really liked the song it was put out on the B-side, and then duly forgotten about until the tour, when it was dusted down for encores. Even though it was not released at all in the States the song was still received really well. When the band were invited to appear at the MTV awards in Los Angeles in 1988 everyone expected them to play one of their hit singles, maybe 'Animal' or 'Pour Some Sugar On Me'. But the band had other ideas. Instead they unleashed 'Tear It Down' to an ecstatic response. In the following days they received an unprecedented amount of mail concerning the track and even their record company were enquiring about it. The song even got into the Top Five on some radio station charts on requests alone. 'You've got to understand that fifteen million had bought the album but only one hundred and fifty thousand the single,' reasoned Joe. 'So potentially over fourteen and a half million hadn't heard it.'

The song was just too good and too popular to let it slip through the net again. They then stripped it down and restructured it during the *Adrenalize* sessions. Obviously, having spent three years preparing the album, the inclusion of 'Tear It Down' left Def Leppard open to dissension from fans and critics alike who thought its inclusion a bit of a cop-out. Joe, although recognizing the discomfort many had with the song's inclusion, explained: 'I know people may say it's bogus giving people stuff that's been out before, but it's a totally new version. If it wasn't included we felt we were ignoring the people that matter most, the audience.'

By the time it hit the racks the waiting period for *Adrenalize* had stretched a little beyond the original intention of just eighteen months. Nevertheless, despite this amazingly long lapse between albums, Def Leppard could still bestride the rock world like the cat that got the cream. The success of *Hysteria* had been incredible, and the tour which didn't end until 1989 had kept them in the public eye for most of that period. By the time *Hysteria* had been released Bon Jovi had challenged with their impressive *Slippery When Wet* album and had soared above Leppard, only for Leppard to return to clip Jovi's wings.

In the spring of 1992, however, there was no threat. Only Guns N' Roses had achieved any sizeable success in the absence of Leppard with the two bands vying for America's Number One position in 1988. But since then Guns N' Roses themselves had been delayed in the studio recording their *Use Your Illusion* albums. Since the release of those records six months previously the LA rockers had gone in a subtly different direction.

Joe was to admit the delays were a small irritation. 'In a perfect world, maybe putting an album out every three years would have been a bit more fun, but I don't know whether the albums would have been as good.' The ideal of putting qualtiy product out rather than quantity was still the prime motivation in the Leppard camp. 'If we put out stuff every four years to the quality of *Pyromania*, *Hysteria*, and now *Adrenalize*, 'cos I do think the new one is as good if not better, then I don't really mind that much. To me the albums are for ever whereas release dates are things that people forget about.'

But what Def Leppard couldn't forget was that they still had a vacancy in their ranks. Since the band had been built on a twin-guitar front they saw no reason to change that now. All they had to do was find the right man.

CHAPTER FOURTEEN

ROCK AROUND
THE WORLD

Once *Adrenalize* was out of the way Def Leppard were on the look out for a second guitarist, especially with an up-coming tour virtually upon them. John Sykes, despite his visit to the studio while work was in progress, was, for betting folk, now considered a rank outsider. The fact that he had also set about working on his own act, Blue Murder, and their second album pretty much ruled him out of the game.

As so much had been staked on Sykes other names were slow to emerge. Def Leppard then did something they had never done before. They held auditions for the post. More specifically, when in LA the band invited six guitarists down to a studio to gauge them both as musicians but more importantly as people. They would be on tour for the foreseeable future and did not want an unstable character who would have to be constantly monitored, as Steve had been on his last excursion. The very location of the auditions also led to many cries of derision. The mere fact that these trials were being held in the USA surely meant that the band had been unable to locate a suitable British guitarist and had scurried off across the Atlantic to recruit the latest whiz-kid hotshot. This did not go down well with the fans. Suddenly the Leppards were on the verge of another major sell-out scam. They hadn't been subjected to this kind of abuse for over a decade. But then they largely brought this one down on their own heads. After their promises of finding a Briton to fill the vacancy, they had now, apparently, opted for a foreigner. To a xenophobic British press this was the most unpatriotic move the band could have made.

But all these accusations were flying about without a hint of fact to back them up. No one but Leppard knew the identity of those turning up for those auditions, and no announcement was due until the fortunate candidate had been fully enrolled. Anything else was mere speculation. But then that never stopped anyone before.

Time, though, was not being kind to Def Leppard. The rock world had lost one of its most effervescent stars, Queen frontman Freddie Mercury, to AIDS the previous year. A special tribute gig to Mercury had been announced on 12th February 1992 at the annual Brits awards show, the equivalent to the American Grammys. The proceeds would go to international AIDS research and the show would feature some of the biggest names in the business. Just how big nobody knew, but that didn't stop all the tickets for the Wembley Stadium show selling out within hours. Before too long the names of the performers were beginning to be made public. The superstars of the music world were all present: Elton John, George Michael, David Bowie, Lisa Stansfield, and Liza Minelli would all contribute, alongside the harder-edged fraternity also keen to lend their services: Metallica, Extreme, Guns N' Roses . . . and Def Leppard.

The speculation began anew. Now, surely, to be able to execute their commitment Leppard must have secured a new guitarist. Leppard confirmed that the position had been filled and that he would be unveiled at Wembley. However, secrets don't stay secret for long in the music biz and a little detective work soon unearthed the name of the musician who had been employed initially to undertake the forthcoming tour. Once his name had been revealed in the press Def Leppard were pretty much forced to announce formally that Vivian Campbell would be Steve Clark's replacement.

As it turned out, Vivian Campbell answered favourably all

the requirements Leppard had asked for. He held a British passport, he was born in Ulster, and had a *curriculum vitae* second to none.

Vivian Campbell had started his career in the early '80s with a local Irish band named Sweet Savage who had captured something of a following on the club circuit. The band's main attempt at securing a shot at the big time came when they were given the support slot on Thin Lizzy's 1982 British tour to promote the *Renegade* album. Despite this tour going well, Sweet Savage seemed destined for the eternal small-tour scene. Campbell was just twenty-one but had big ambitions. He obviously felt he wasn't fulfilling his potential and later even admitted to a sneaking admiration for Phil Collen's old band, Girl, so much so that when news broke that Phil had left Girl to join Def Leppard, Vivian audaciously gave Girl frontman Phil Lewis a call to ask for an audition. But this idea was rejected. Lewis had tired of the perpetual criticism levelled at the band and had joined forces with former Gillan guitarist Bernie Tormé to front a new act.

Former Rainbow bassist Jimmy Bain was, at that time, in the throes of putting a band together with fellow ex-Rainbow and Black Sabbath vocalist Ronnie James Dio. Still requiring a guitar player for the project, Bain saw the potential of the young man when he caught Sweet Savage on that Lizzy tour. He was invited down to London to jam with the embryo band, and made such a good impression he was immediately invited to join. Supplemented by the drumming of Vinnie Appice, who had also been in Black Sabbath with Dio, the band was launched under the title Dio and relocated to Los Angeles where they recorded their début album. Released in June 1983, Dio's *Holy Diver* was to stand tall amongst the competition. It integrated a classic rock sound with an up-tempo vibe and garnered critical acclaim from all corners. The album has since become a classic of the Hard Rock genre.

Dio went on to make their live début on one of the world's biggest stages, that year's Castle Donington 'Monsters of Rock' festival. Although appearing well down on a bill also featuring headliners Whitesnake as well as ZZ Top and Meat Loaf, Dio garnered great accolades, many considering them to be 'Band of the Day'. Unfortunately, from *Holy Diver* onwards Dio were on the slippery slope. In 1984 *Last in Line* received a good reception, but by 1985's *Sacred Heart* the most charitable description was to be, at best, 'patchy'. Campbell subsequently left, somewhat acrimoniously, to be replaced by ex-Giuffria guitarist Craig Goldy.

The Irishman then disappeared for the next couple of years. Reports of him trying to put his own band together in LA regularly filtered through but nothing concrete ever got off the ground. In 1987 Campbell re-emerged, as a member of Whitesnake. With the *1987* album completed Whitesnake's supremo David Coverdale needed a fresh image for his band. He was not naïve in his commercial approach, he knew that with the onset of the MTV generation he needed a young, good-looking band to back him on the videos. Vivian therefore was enrolled to pose in the background for the 'Still of the Night' video shoot. Coverdale had also enrolled Adrian Vandenburg in the other guitarist slot with Rudy Sarzo on bass and Tommy Aldridge on drums. Despite their expertise the star of the video was Coverdale's girlfriend Tawny Kittaen who managed to drape herself around Coverdale and his car. Nevertheless, in one video Coverdale had captured the imagination of the youth. *1987* was to become the biggest-selling Whitesnake album ever.

Vivian was duly enrolled for the duration of the tour alongside the other video stars, even if they hadn't actually played a note on the record. Sadly Campbell didn't get the chance to record with Whitesnake. During pre-production for the follow up, *Slip Of The Tongue*, Campbell and Coverdale parted company. With Adrian Vandenberg sustaining a hand injury, all guitars on *Slip Of The Tongue* were performed by Steve Vai.

Even before Coverdale had given Vivian his marching orders, the Irishman had moved into the field of production and was involved particularly with a rock-based blues outfit called The Riverdogs who were resident in LA. Having lost his position in the 'Snake camp, Vivian stepped out from behind the production console to join the band as full-time member. It gave him the chance to branch out once more into areas he rarely entertained, such as writing and being free to express himself without any restraints. The Riverdogs' début album failed to set the world alight.

Undeterred, Vivian was still chasing his rock 'n' roll dream, and his next port of call was to be with another vocalist of worldwide renown. Lou Gramm had been the singer with AOR gods Foreigner. Gramm had left the band after inner friction with guitarist and band leader Mick Jones following a down turn in the band's fortunes and arguments over the direction the band should follow.

Together, Vivian and Gramm teamed up along with Kevin Valentine and Bruce Turgon. Naming their new group Shadowking, the quartet were soon signed to the Atlantic label, where Gramm had enjoyed all his success with the Foreigner albums and a couple of solo outings. With its lavish AOR/rock style the eponymous album received rave reviews and at last Campbell seemed on the verge of success in his own right. Atlantic didn't quite see it that way, though. Many people believed that the label signed the band on Lou Gramm's pedigree and when Foreigner-sized sales figures failed to materialize they lost interest and refused to put any more money into the project. So uninterested were they that it was left to the American Dream Promotions to bring the band over to Britain for a one-off appearance at the London Astoria as part of their weekly showcase of US-based bands. Kevin Valentine soon became disillusioned and left to replace Fred Coury on the drum stool in Cinderella. Whether Shadowking would stay together was open to much speculation, and in December 1991 news filtered through that Campbell had left for destinations unknown. Having been writing songs with Danny Wilde of the Rembrandts, Campbell was, in fact working on his own album in Los Angeles when he got a call asking him if he would like to audition for Def Leppard.

It was Gramm who gave the first hints that Vivian might be linked to Leppard: in early April 1992 he let slip that the guitarist had been jamming with Def Leppard but didn't know whether Vivian had been invited to join. Lou obviously didn't bear any animosity towards Vivian on his decision to quit Shadowking. But now, at last, Vivian Campbell was about to step up into the big league.

No sooner had Vivian been confirmed as Def Leppard's new guitarist than the rehearsals for the tour began. But the Freddie Mercury tribute show loomed ominously close. Rather than throw Vivian straight into the media circus surrounding the Wembley show, Def Leppard decided to test out just how they would gel on stage by playing a small club called McGonagle's in the heart of Dublin. The hot and sweaty atmosphere of the club gave the Irishman a baptism of fire, which, by general consensus, he carried off admirably.

Leppard then readied themselves for one of the biggest concerts the world had seen since Live Aid back in the summer of 1985. The plan was relatively simple. Metallica, Extreme, Def Leppard, and Guns N' Roses would warm up the crowd with sets lasting twenty minutes. Following this the remaining trio from Queen would perform the band's hits fronted by guest vocalists with guest musicians coming on to lend their expertise. To this end the cast was required to turn up for rehearsals at a studio in Brays, near Wembley, where the set and who would contribute to which track was decided.

Held on 20th April 1992, the concert had captivated the world media in advance. The nature of Mercury's death coupled with this benefit concert would be the ideal vehicle to bring home to the youth of the world that AIDS was an indiscriminate disease that could affect anyone if they were foolish enough to ignore the warnings. The 72,000 tickets had sold out in hours and an estimated 1.5 billion viewers would see the concert beamed live around the world on TV.

After a brief introduction by former Queen members Brian May, Roger Taylor, and John Deacon, Metallica took to the stage, pummelling the crowd with their unique brand of Heavy Metal. It was to the next band up that the crowd, warmed up by Metallica, really seemed to respond. Introduced by May as the band closer than anyone to the ethic of Queen, Extreme concentrated their set on a montage of Queen's hits which earned them an ecstatic response, throwing in their own huge hit, 'More Than Words', for good measure. The gauntlet was thrown down for Leppard to follow.

As fate would have it, Leppard never really seemed to come close. Their brief set was delayed when, remarkably, Rick Allen's drum kit went missing! Vital as the kit is to Leppard the band had to kick their heels while it was located. By the time Leppard were introduced by Roger Taylor the euphoria of Extreme's set had dissipated leaving the crowd somewhat cold once more. Most would agree that Leppard couldn't really get them moving again until the end of their set. Resplendent in Union Jack strides Joe Elliott entered with: 'A bit of rock 'n' roll music for ya!' as the band launched into 'Animal' followed by the soon to be staple 'Let's Get Rocked'. Obviously all eyes were on the new recruit, and Vivian seemed to be enjoying himself just fine, as were the rest of the band. The only discordant note, most people agreed, was not a musical one at all. But what was going to take some getting used to was the new guitarist's brown hair! And Def Leppard, after all, had been largely blond for some considerable time. But undoubtedly the pinnacle of Leppard's slot was the appearance on stage for the first time in a musical role of Brian May, who joined the band for a rousing version of Queen's 1975 hit, 'Now I'm Here'.

Following another interminable delay for the spoof Metal of Spinal Tap, Guns N' Roses took to the stage to a rapturous welcome. However, due to the previous delays the Gunners were forced to cut short their set, a decision that they graciously accepted in keeping with the meaning of the show. As the evening began to spread its darkness across the stadium, the Queen trio took to the stage for their largely anticipated final performance. Cranking into the near Heavy Metal tune 'Tie

Your Mother Down', Brian May took vocals for the first verse before Joe Elliott appeared to take over. Guns N' Roses' Slash also joined the scene for the triumphant celebration of Freddie Mercury's music which was to take place over the next two and a half hours until proceedings came to a grand fnale with singer and AIDS campaigner Liza Minelli taking the lead for 'We Are The Champions'. As she did so the whole ensemble gathered onstage as a massive all-star choir. The event had been a huge success.

While the press reported an enthusiastic response to the gig, Def Leppard's performance met with a lukewarm reception. Metallica also met with some criticism, but not necessarily for their three numbers. Their contribution to the event, 'Enter Sandman', 'Sad But True', and 'Nothing Else Matters', were recorded live and were being rushed out as a single!

When the dust had settled on the Mercury gig word from the Leppard camp seemed to suggest that the show, in all honesty, wasn't one of their best. But the reasons behind them agreeing to appear far outnumbered those negative aspects of their performance.

But Def Leppard pressed on and began their world tour with a batch of low-key dates across Europe. These would be the real test of the new guitarist. His musical ability was not in question, so what this first leg of dates aimed at was to introduce him to the fans but, more importantly, it would decide whether he would fit into the band on a personal level. After being nursemaids to Steve Clark for much of the previous tour, the last thing the band wanted was another unreliable, disruptive member within their close-knit ranks.

It had been a long time since Leppard had set foot on European soil to play live so the dilemma facing manager Peter Mensch was how to promote the tour without being seen to be over-anxious. Given the small scale of the venues, had Leppard been observed as advertising heavily then this could have been misinterpreted as their having difficulty selling out the venues. If, on the other hand, they kept the gigs a big secret and no one had shown up then Leppard would have been splashed all over the media under derogatory headlines proclaiming their early demise due to lack of pulling power. As it turned out, Mensch needn't have worried. The shows, which stretched usually to two hours in length, were all sold out and everyone went home satisfied. Not least Vivian, who was fitting in better than anyone could have hoped for. He was relishing his new role, and making sure he was very vocal in letting everyone know that he was having the time of his life.

Along with Vivian, Leppard also had a few other slight changes to their touring line up both technically and in personnel. On the technical side, the Sony guitars that had to be heavily modified for the 'in the round' sets had been dropped in favour of Nady guitars which were more specific in their duties. Joe also had a new earpiece which acted as a small monitor. When they returned from the clubs to playing 'in the round' the earpiece would have the desired effect of keeping him in check with exactly what was going on at all times instead of the previous situation where he was experiencing brief dropouts of sound as he moved into 'dead areas' about the stage. On the personnel front, Malvin Mortimer, who had acted as Steve Clark's guitar technician on the *Hysteria* jaunt, now found himself elevated to the position of tour manager. Mortimer is better known for his sterling vocal contribution on the B-side of the 'Rocket' single as well as the later Stumpus Maximus promo single. Mortimer found himself a star in Greece of all places for his hideous rendition of the track. The Greeks had flipped the single over, making 'Release Me' the A-side and in doing so converting Mortimer into a Top Ten artist!

As the club tour got under way at the beginning of May, dates were announced in the UK, starting the British leg on 21st June at Glasgow SECC. Such was the demand for tickets that many shows were added before the dates began. From Glasgow, Def Leppard would play their hometown Sheffield Arena before moving on to London's Earl's Court and finally three dates at the NEC in Birmingham. For the first time in

Britain these dates would be conducted 'in the round'. The venues had been especially selected for their capacity to put on such a show, but what made this trek a little easier was that a new rig had been built at the Docklands Arena in London. This new rig was constructed out of aluminium and therefore was a lot lighter than their old rig which would have brought the venues' roofs down under its weight.

As an appetizer for the tour the second single from the album was released. 'Make Love Like A Man' continued Leppard's run of success, acquiring both airplay and a respectable chart position. Curiously enough, the track had been banned in Korea for being too sexually provocative! *Adrenalize* was released there with just nine tracks as a result.

Keeping up Leppard's British traditions, a Scottish band named Gun were named as support act. It was thought the Scots' brand of commercial Hard Rock would be the perfect opener for the Leppards with a sound to complement their own. In all respects the tour was a massive success, with Def Leppard garnering rave reviews for their lengthy, well-paced two-hour extravaganza while Gun went down well, and introduced themselves to a new audience despite having to come to terms with the four-sided stage.

With its spring release, *Adrenalize* sparked off many new rumours that the band would return to headline the Castle Donington Festival. These rumours were dispelled by the band themselves who had announced that their huge up-coming American tour would take priority, and thus make the logistics of returning to play the festival a virtual impossibility. In spite of Leppard's denials it wasn't until Iron Maiden were confirmed as the headliners with Skid Row filling the vacant 'Special Guest' spot that their tenuous links with the festival were severed.

Leppard kicked off the North American leg of their 'Seven-Day Weekend' tour safe in the knowledge that all was well on the Western front. *Adrenalize* had gone straight to No. 1 on the *Billboard* charts on the week of release, no mean feat in itself but all the more remarkable considering the opposition. Bruce

Springsteen is a national hero in the States: his blue-collar anthems from such albums as *Born In The USA* and *Born To Run* had long since endeared the New Jersey songsmith to the soul of the American heartland. He was now set to take a leaf out of Guns N' Roses' book by releasing two separate albums on the same day. Unfortunate as it seemed for Leppard, these releases, titled *Human Touch* and *Lucky Town* were scheduled for the same day as *Adrenalize*.

The same problem had nearly befallen Guns N' Roses' *Use Your Illusion* albums and Metallica's *Black Album* a year before, until their respective record companies, Geffen and Polygram, had seen the benefits of rescheduling. No such agreement seemed forthcoming between the Leppard and Springsteen labels. Each felt they had the best shot and no inch was given in the head-to-head fight for the Number One slot. Of course Leppard won hands down, but in Springsteen's defence it was argued that by having two brand-new albums out on the same day his fans, without a great deal of disposable income, were split on which to buy first. So Leppard won, the Springsteen fans claimed, only by default. Well, possibly, but the plain fact was that Leppard had easily out-sold Springsteen in sheer numbers. What made this success for Leppard all the more ironic was that Springsteen's sister, Pamela, is credited with photography on *Adrenalize*'s back cover.

In spite of the fact that the world recession was biting into the markets and having adverse effects on the concert-going public Leppard were making considerable headway on this tour. Bon Jovi, their nearest musical rivals, appeared to be having a lean time on the circuit due to the onset of the tougher, more direct sound of the Grunge genre becoming increasingly popular amongst American teenagers. Def Leppard, though, seemed to slide through unhindered.

The new guitarist had slipped easily into the Leppard entourage. Joe had said earlier in the tour that Vivian had exceeded all expectations, labelling the Irishman a 'perfect fit', meeting all the band's requirements.

As with any undertaking of this size – taking fifty-eight people out on the road for two years – the tour wasn't without its hiccups. In Bismark, North Dakota, on 5th September, with a sell-out 8,500 crowd going nuts Joe had to stop the show midway through as the front rows were being crushed. This scenario is bad enough in normal circumstances but it was compounded by the fact that Leppard were both playing 'in the round' and so all four front rows were being crushed, and that it was an unseated venue. Fortunately, no one was seriously hurt and the gig finished without further incident, apart from two youngsters who had to be told that their parents had been hurt in a serious car accident. Putting this behind them, less than a week later, on 9th September, Leppard appeared at the MTV awards in Los Angeles once again. This time they were nominated four times but actually won in none of their categories. To make up for their disappointment at losing out on an award Leppard played live once again, this time treating the audience to the now rather better known 'Let's Get Rocked'. Sixteen thousand at Salt Lake City, Utah, and a rabid reaction to the first show they'd played in Yakima, Washington, more than made up for any disappointment.

As fortune would have it, the band were booked to play Landover, Maryland, on 3rd November. Nothing unusual about this as a rule, but Landover is situated by the capital city of Washington, DC, and 3rd November was the date set for the American presidential election. Special monitors were set up on the stage so that Joe could relay information about the progress of the candidates to the crowd. With much of the crowd supporting the independent candidate Ross Perot, when Joe announced: 'There's a new sheriff in town and he goes by the name of Bill Clinton' this news was not received enthusiastically. The gig had been going really well until this point, but the news of Clinton's election only served to dissipate the atmosphere. Undeterred, Leppard played the only encore fitting of the occasion, a cover of Alice Cooper's 'Elected' with Joe resplendent in a Stars and Stripes outfit. The damage caused by the

Clinton victory was too much for Leppard to save and the band were more than happy to call it quits at the end of the night.

Pittsburgh, Pennsylvania, posed difficulties of a different sort. Having promised that they would play all dates on this leg of the tour 'in the round', the Pittsburgh date was put in jeopardy when it became clear that Leppard were faced with the choice of either playing at one end of the venue or cancelling. This being a Leppard stronghold the possibility of cancelling would have been a really depressing option to take. One of the Q Prime management team, though, had heard that Neil Diamond had played the very same venue with a transportable support system. After some detective work and serious negotiation Def Leppard hired the rig, at a not insubstantial sum, and the gig went ahead as planned.

During the flight from Pittsburgh Joe's health suddenly took an agonizing turn for the worse. A sharp pain hit him right across his chest rendering the singer virtually paralysed with pain. At first it was thought that he'd had a heart attack, the pain was that severe. At the tender age of thirty-three this diagnosis seemed unlikely. As the flight progressed the pain moved into his back. This at least relieved the anxiety about a possible heart attack but as soon as the plane landed he was admitted to hospital for a series of checks. The good news was that his heart was fine but the bad news was that he'd contracted pleurisy, a lung inflammation. Prescribed sixteen tablets a day and told to take it very easy for the next week, Joe did the exact opposite and headed straight to the next venue, where he managed to complete the gig, albeit in abject pain.

This debilitating illness was to stay with Joe for some while. With no time off to rid himself of the problem the pleurisy took hold and refused to be shaken. Unsurprisingly, he experienced breathing problems, virtually fatal in an artistic sense to a singer. All the pressure was put on his vocal cords which, in time, also began to give out under the strain. But Leppard, being old troupers, insisted that the show must go on, and it did, Joe eventually returning to full health and full voice a few weeks later than originally expected.

In spite of Joe's vocal problems the gigs were going down the proverbial storm with the fans. Introducing 'White Lightning', Joe would blow a kiss towards heaven in memory of Steve. Elsewhere, both Phil and Vivian were having fun, both executing solo spots which would invariably ape classic rock tunes. Phil could be heard cranking out the riff to AC/DC's 'Back in Black' whereas Vivian would whack out a lampoon of Metallica's thunderous 'Enter Sandman'.

In the band's absence from Britain, the record company hadn't been altogether idle. In September they'd released the third single from the album. The ballad 'Have You Ever Needed Someone So Bad' kept Leppard in the charts and never far from the public eye. Then, at the beginning of December, in an effort to boost *Adrenalize*'s sales in the Christmas rush, Phonogram issued the album as a special picture disc edition.

Following a brief respite for Christmas, the band were back on the road in North America, capitalizing on the upward surge in sales in that region which were now nearing the three million mark. Britain once again had to make do with another single. This time it was 'Heaven Is'. There were also rumours beginning, as is traditional at that time of year, concerning the large outdoor festivals due to take place the following summer. Once again, Leppard were cited alongside Aerosmith as prime candidates for the headlining slot at Donington. It soon became apparent that this coming summer would see a plethora of festivals both in Britain and in Europe. No words of confirmation would be forthcoming on these festivals for a couple of months at least, but speculation was rife that Def Leppard would feature very heavily on the summer's festival circuit.

In February 1993, a few of Leppard's summer dates in Europe began trickling through. The first inkling Britain got of these dates was the advertisements in the national rock press offering jaunts to Paris for a gig at the Zenith Arena on 14th

May. This signalled the start of the Leppard name being dropped whenever a festival was mentioned. Obviously Castle Donington, which was uncharacteristically late in finalizing a bill, topped everyone's tips, but as the date drew nearer the likelihood was that Leppard would play a large outdoor festival in their own right.

As predicted, the glut of rock festivals became a reality. Guns N' Roses announced two dates at the Milton Keynes Bowl on the weekend of 28th May. Bruce Springsteen was also to play there the week before and a week later Metallica announced a date at the very same venue. The annual Glastonbury Festival held in late June promised the appearance of such legendary figures as Robert Plant, The Kinks, and The Velvet Underground alongside the younger generation of rock icons such as The Black Crowes and Lenny Kravitz. The inaugural Phoenix Festival, concentrating on the rock hopefuls such as Sonic Youth, Faith No More, the Manic Street Preachers, and once again the Black Crowes, was also pencilled into diaries. Bon Jovi also announced dates, yet again, at the Milton Keynes Bowl in mid-September on the back of European audiences accepting their last album *Keep The Faith* with far more open arms than their American counterparts.

With all this activity scheduled for the coming months, Leppard were faced with a dilemma. Not just where to play but when so as not adversely to affect their pulling potential. The main contender seemed to be Wembley Stadium. It was easily accessible and had fewer gigs booked there during the course of the year. Indeed, at one stage news was leaked that the gig would take place at Wembley with Mötley Crüe appearing as special guests. But this wasn't so much 'news' as idle speculation.

Eventually the decision was taken to make use of another proposed venue, the Don Valley Stadium in Def Leppard's home town of Sheffield. The deciding factor in choosing this venue was not only because it was close to home but because in 1993 Sheffield was celebrating its centenary. The only question mark over the site was the fact that, being renowned as a top athletics arena, this would be the first rock festival it had held. Other possible venues in the city included both soccer stadiums, Hillsborough and Brammell Lane – homes to the rival clubs Wednesday and United – but with supporters of both sides in the entourage the neutral turf of Don Valley was considered the best option. The contenders for supporting cast still featured Mötley Crüe, a band who had also gone through a fair amount of turmoil. Crüe had lost their original vocalist, Vince Neil, a year before and had recruited John Corabi from fellow LA outfit The Scream. Crüe had been working on their first album with Corabi and the prospect of getting the band on the bill for their Corabi-led British début would have been worth at least an extra 10,000 people on the gate. The announcement of Don Valley also ended any likelihood that the Donington festival would take place. Aerosmith were still putting the finishing touches to their forthcoming *Get A Grip* album, which ruled them out of contention. So with Leppard, Guns N' Roses, and Metallica all playing alternative venues, Donington had to bow to the inevitable and cancel the event due to the lack of a merited headliner.

Meanwhile Def Leppard were still trekking around the States. The band were massive football fans, and they were being kept in touch with their supported teams with videos mailed out to them. By either fate or good fortune Joe's and Rick's beloved Sheffield United and Rick Savage's Sheffield Wednesday won through to the brink of the annual prestige English footballing event, the FA Cup semi-finals. As luck would have it the Sheffield clubs were paired against each other, the day of judgement being 3rd April. Unfortunately for the boys in the band, they were scheduled to be playing in Canada that night and the tour itinerary was so tight that the group couldn't afford the time to allow Joe and Sav to fly back to England, so the boys couldn't see the game in the flesh. At their insistence a hotel had to be found which could provide them with a satellite link-up for the game: a painstaking search found the ideal place. In England, the game was so important it had been relocated to the home of British football, Wembley Stadium, with the kick-off to take place at midday. With the time difference the Leppard crew had to sit up through the night in order to see the game. After a typically hard-fought local derby, the game was decided only in extra time when Wednesday beat United 2–1 to reach their first final for many years. Sav enjoyed the delight of victory and Joe had to suffer the jibes endured by any fan when his side suffers an ignominious defeat. Sav was to feel the same heartache when Wednesday eventually lost the final after a replay to North London's Arsenal. A defeat that rubbed salt into the wounds, as Wednesday had also lost the Coca Cola Cup Final to the same opponents two months earlier. Such is the devotion soccer inspires!

In May Def Leppard crisscrossed Europe playing both to their own audiences and those of the large outdoor festivals. Spain, Portugal, France, Belgium, the Netherlands, Switzerland, all received the attentions of Def Leppard and, on their own dates and selected festivals, that of the band who had continued on from supporting Leppard through North America, Ugly Kid Joe. They were a band of American teenagers who had taken their name in ridicule of glamsters Pretty Boy Floyd. They had released their début album, *America's Least Wanted*, on the back of a massive hit single, '(I Hate) Everything About You', taken from their first EP. The band took the image of rowdy college boys to increasing extremes, and in doing so, especially on the back of teen rock films such as *Wayne's World* and *Bill and Ted's Excellent Adventure*, had captured a spirit of rebellion in the American youth. Now, they were bringing their blend of serious rock tinged with the comic asides to Europe. Judging by the charts they were doing a very good job.

However, in some places Def Leppard weren't gaining the sell outs which were by now almost obligatory: in Copenhagen only 4,000 of the 6,500 tickets were sold. Over breakfast the next morning the Leppard camp was in frivolous mood as they entertained their guest Robert Plant – who had been invited on stage for the encores the previous night where he and Leppard ravaged through Led Zeppelin's 'Black Dog', 'Rock and Roll', and 'Whole Lotta Love' – by hiring an Egyptian belly dancer/stripper to perform her party-piece.

The less than full houses were caused by the massive tours-cum-festivals doing the rounds. U2 had roped in huge audiences with their wide appeal, while the packages put together by Guns N' Roses and Metallica, who were supported by the likes of Brian May, The Cult, Megadeth, Soul Asylum, Suicidal Tendencies, and The Almighty, had sponged up the rest of the market. All things considered Leppard were doing admirably just holding their own in the face of the competition.

Bad news greeted the party when they arrived in Sweden, however. Former David Bowie guitarist Mick Ronson, Joe's teenage idol and latter-day good friend, had lost his long, hard-fought battle against cancer. To his memory, at that night's show in Stockholm, Def Leppard played an acoustic version of 'Ziggy Stardust' and later, as a last encore, 'Slaughter On Tenth Avenue'. The sense of loss was made all the deeper as Joe had recently recorded a couple of tracks with Ronson for the guitarist's forthcoming solo album.

The Rock AM Ring Festival in Germany was to provide the biggest crowd Leppard played to throughout the whole 'Seven-Day Weekend' tour. Fifty-five thousand piled in to see Leppard headline the event above such luminaries as The Black Crowes and Robert Plant as well as a host of other diverse acts. Having previously gone through a long bout of less than complimentary remarks between The Crowes and themselves, conducted via the pages of the international rock press, the Leppards were more than happy to sit down and chat with their contemporaries in the Crowes camp, which served to call a truce between the bands.

Sadly, it was not this informal peace meeting that gained the press coverage, nor even their performing on stage. Rather, the pages were filled with the sensationalism of a confrontation between the Leppard camp and leader of the band Danzig, Glenn Danzig. Insults were apparently traded backstage with

Joe, Viv, and Phil uncharacteristically ready to pile in and sort the affair out. The situation was calmed down before the two sides could come to blows, but the accusations flew for months in the press.

So, what with one thing and another, Leppard were glad to get home and play Sheffield again. Although they were looking forward to this date probably more than any other on the tour, there was a fair amount of consternation within the camp regarding whether they would bring the whole festival off successfully. Guns N' Roses had played Milton Keynes the week before, and the fact that Metallica were also playing the Bowl, over two hundred miles from Sheffield, on Saturday 5th June, just the day before, meant that fans whose loyalties crossed musical boundaries had to make a difficult choice of which gig to attend. Leppard's ploy of adding Mötley Crüe to the bill had not proved successful as their album was taking a lot longer than anticipated, so they were still in the studio on the other side of the world. Other problems reared up on the question of transport available to the crowd to and from the venue. Being England, on a Sunday the rail network shuts down early with the last timetabled train likely to leave Sheffield before the end of the gig. And naturally, being England, there was always the possibility of inclement weather.

The bill, therefore, took a very predictable turn. Beginning proceedings would be another band who had originated in the locality, Terrorvision. Having been signed by EMI, Terrorvision were busying themselves promoting their recently re-released *Formaldehyde* album which had already spawned a couple of near-hit singles. Maintaining their sequence of appearances as regular support, the next band to take the stage would be Ugly Kid Joe. Replacing Mötley Crüe came South London rockers Thunder. Don Valley would be the British début for their new Swedish bassist Michael Hoglund. While the majority of fans were disappointed at the absence of Mötley Crüe, the confirmation of Thunder was greeted with a good deal of applause from those attending. Thunder had risen out of the now defunct

Terraplane with their classy début album, *Back Street Symphony*, gaining rave reviews for their combination of influences such as Bad Company and Free entwined with their own slant on the rock genre. They had earned themselves the 'Band of the Day' tag when they appeared in the opening slot at the 1991 Castle Donington festival and had bolstered their reputation with their second album, *Laughing on Judgement Day*. On the down side of this was the fact that they had toured heavily over the past couple of years and would therefore present little in the way of surprises for the crowd.

With a hundred and fifteen people hired to produce the gig, Don Valley got under way seven minutes earlier than planned with Terrorvision going on stage in glorious sunshine just before four o'clock in the afternoon, in front of a capacity 40,000 audience. The transport difficulties weren't as severe as first thought due to the fact that 80 per cent of tickets sold were bought by people within a small radius of Sheffield. Each of the support bands acquitted themselves admirably. While Terrorvision at the very least retained the attention of the crowd, Ugly Kid Joe's front man Whitfield Crane stole the show with his on-stage impressions, raps, and climbs up the scaffolding, while Thunder produced a powerful, if slightly predictable, set.

Basking in the hot sun all day had reduced the crowd's fervour level quite considerably during the support acts' sets but, at ten past eight, with the sun just gently beginning to slip from the sky, the strains of Joe's query 'Do Ya Wanna Get Rocked?' set the crowd off into a frenzy. With all the members of their family plus the whole of Sheffield watching, Def Leppard pulled out all the stops for the gig of their lives. The set lasted two hours and included solos from both guitarists with Phil being decreed an 'Honorary Yorkshireman' by Joe before his slot. The only sour note of the whole evening came when Joe, picking up an acoustic guitar to go solo with a cover of Springsteen's 'My Home Town', incited the hugely local crowd to join him in the chorus only to be met with indifference, forcing him back into the bosom of the band for 'Two Steps

Behind', this being the acoustic ballad that Leppard had contributed to film star Arnold Schwarzenegger's latest movie, *The Last
Action Hero*. The film failed to live up to its blockbuster billing,
but the rock soundtrack was greeted far more favourably. Other
artists who had contributed tracks were Megadeth, Queensryche, Anthrax, and Tesla as well as giants such as Aerosmith
and AC/DC. For the video to accompany AC/DC's 'Big Guns',
Schwarzenegger proved himself a true rock fan by making an
appearance in which he evolved into an over-grown (AC/DC
guitarist) Angus Young figure, schoolboy garb included, and
proceeded to ape the diminutive rock star's every move!

The gig went down a storm with the band, fans and press
alike. Before the gig Joe had stated: 'We just need to grow a big
pair of balls to do it!' And the balls, clearly, duly appeared.
Otherwise, one of the few criticisms of the set list was that the
only track that predated *Pyromania* was 'Another Hit And Run',
and considering the location it was felt that a couple of early
tunes wouldn't have gone amiss. At the climax of the tour the
band looked back on the Don Valley show not only as the
highlight of the 'Seven-Day Weekend' tour but as a highlight,
thus far, of Def Leppard's whole career. For Sav it was the icing
on the cake for the band who had begun life just down the road
sixteen years earlier, a realization of exactly how far the band
had come.

After the euphoria of 'Relative City', the next point of call
was Japan, and directly afterwards a return through the United
States for the duration of the summer concentrating on the
outdoor amphitheatres, and in particular attempting to play the
areas that had been overlooked on the last leg of the tour.

Talk was also emerging at this time regarding the possibility
of another album release before the end of the year. During the
Hysteria jaunt speculation had arisen as to the imminent arrival
of a boxed set which would compromise live tracks, B-sides, and
out-takes. This idea was given the cold shoulder when the tour
was lengthened to accommodate demand, but this time news
broke that the band were working on songs while out on the

road for a single album full of B-sides and rarities which would, in effect, serve as a tribute to Steve Clark. But, given Leppard's history of perfecting their recorded works, no one really felt this album would see the light of day at least until the middle of 1994.

With *Adrenalize* now nearing the six-million sales mark, the pressure to deliver was all but off and Leppard were now having a ball out on stage. The massive production had been pruned down, no longer were they playing 'in the round', no longer was there an extravagant light show. This was the bare bones of the band on show and it resulted in the band enjoying themselves enormously. That is apart from when one of their massive trucks went missing *en route* to a show in Las Cruces, New Mexico. As it contained six tons of equipment worth over $750,000, the show had to be put back by one day to allow new gear to be flown in to enable the rescheduled show to go ahead. The truck was found a couple of days later in Tucson, Arizona, with all the gear accounted for.

On 1st September, the town mayor of Fargo, North Dakota, declared the day 'Def Leppard Day'! The local radio station blared out Leppard tunes all day while the band left their handprints in the Fargo Walk of Fame. Then came a huge shock to those who doubted that it was possible: the announcement that Def Leppard would indeed be releasing a new album, even earlier than originally planned. *Retro Active* would see the light of day on 4th October. Comprising re-recorded cuts from the band's history, it would be much more a fans/collectors piece than anything else; the important point was that it had been recorded and completed while the band had been out on the road.

The 'Seven-Day Weekend' tour had far outlasted its billing. In all, two hundred and forty-one dates had been played over seventeen months, ending in the last week of September with a triumphant gig in Mexico City. So many tickets were sold for the final gigs that, despite the stage being set at one end of the indoor arena, the band were forced to play an impromptu 'in the round' set by the promoters who opened up the seats at the rear of the stage to allow all 20,000 available seats to be used. By this stage the set list had been changed around yet again. The band would begin the set with 'Rock! Rock! (Till You Drop)', and alter the running order slightly from that which featured on the European jaunt, 'Let's Get Rocked' sliding into an encore position. But despite the imminent arrival of *Retro Active* only 'Two Steps Behind' from that album featured in the set. Eventually the tour wound down to its inevitable conclusion.

During the tour Leppard had played to an incredible figure, over two million fans, trawling eleven trucks weighing an astonishing fifty-eight tons to transport the gear in their wake. The roadies had to handle forty-four guitars, including three belonging to Joe, replacing nearly 25,000 strings in the process. Over 800 drumsticks were used by Rick and those with just one arm! The band managed to fly the equivalent of eight times around the world just in travelling between gigs in the States. The sound system blasted out 100,000 watts of music. The largest audience the band played to was the 55,000 in Germany, the smallest was a mere 200 at the Molson Log Cabin Party in Canada. And if ever sustenance was needed the backstage catering crew estimated that the number of meals they dished up on the tour was nearing 12,000!

Vivian had made a great impression on his first trek. His guitar playing was equal to Steve's, but his vocals were far stronger, adding a new depth to the backing line. The confident Irishman had been heard to utter statements that he knew he was the best man for the job and that he was enjoying himself fully, mainly because he felt much more at home and freer to express himself within Def Leppard. The band were equally happy to have him along as he could be relied upon not to fall flat on his face when he entered a room, which added to the relaxed atmosphere of the tour and resulted in the whole caboodle running a lot more smoothly.

Their haul across the world was extensive and exhausting

but they had broken in their new guitarist and played to more people than ever before. Right now it seemed an appropriate moment to take a little time out, to rest and relax and just let an album do the talking for them.

CHAPTER FIFTEEN

ROLL THE CREDITS

On 4th October 1993, the *Retro Active* package was released. The album's first point of note was its rawer sound. It was still unquestionably a product from the Leppard stable, but it was also a giant step away in production technique from their previous offerings. This was no surprise when the exact nature of the recording process became known. All the tracks had been reworked while the band were out on the 'Seven-Day Weekend' tour. The majority of the recording had been done within nine days at Joe Elliott's studio in Dublin, but constraints in time forced them to work on other parts while out on the road. However, huge advances in technology had meant that small portable studios, the size of a suitcase, had been devised that would be far easier to transport through the tour. This meant the band could work on their parts in their own time, either in hotels or just while twiddling their thumbs backstage during soundchecks.

The idea for a project of this kind had begun after they'd been asked to contribute a track to *The Last Action Hero*'s soundtrack. When they finished 'Two Steps Behind' while on tour it gave rise to the idea that it might be possible to complete a whole album in the same fashion. The album, which had been first thought out with the members just kicking around ideas, began to take on a sense of purpose during the first few months of 1993. When they finally got down to the recording, the album took just under four months to finish, from May to August.

Retro Active has a track listing of thirteen songs. However, allowing the album to play out its run reveals an extra track tagged on to the end of the album. This is the third version of 'Miss You In A Heartbeat', this one performed simply by Joe sitting at his piano, reciting the ballad in its purest form. The first track on the album is 'Desert Song', a song originated by Steve Clark way back in 1984. The mysticism of the Eastern-tinged swirling hook reminded the listener of Led Zeppelin's forays into the Orient and was therefore too good a song to discard. In 1987 the song was reworked under the working title of 'Into The Light', but it was not to be until the spring of 1993 that Joe found the inspiration for the lyrics. This came from the plight of Mick Ronson whose battle against cancer had finally been lost. The lyrics deal with the isolation felt by one fighting a long, lonely struggle and could also fit with anyone in dire straits.

Although it was the first song to evolve from the *Hysteria* writing sessions, 'Fractured Love' was another number that had been converted to record for the first time. While recording the basic tracks in Dublin during a brief respite in the tour during June, Joe was up for most of the night working on the track, he had to be literally dragged away from the studio at twenty past eight in order to make his flight to Japan on time! 'Fractured Love' had originally been written during the *Hysteria* sessions but instead of using it as a B-side the song was saved as the intro needed working on. The tune was re-arranged but Joe's vocals from 1985 were saved for the version released on the album. He actually sang the first verse down the phone!

Def Leppard have always cited the Glam bands of the mid-'70s as major influences; their brand of commercial pop rock was not lost on the Sheffield lads. Sweet were major players in this movement and along with Slade, T-Rex, and Gary Glitter had a lasting effect on them. Having originally recorded the cover of

Sweet's 'Action' for the 'Make Love Like A Man' flip-side, with a rendition that the band felt was slightly rushed, Rick Allen re-recorded the drum parts, putting real drums over the top of the drum machine, and the backing vocals were re-done with the aim being that the finished version would have a really energetic live feel while retaining the energy of the original. A feat they obviously accomplished as the track went straight into the UK singles charts at Number Twenty-Two in January 1994, rising to Number Thirteen a week later.

The first of the two versions of 'Two Steps Behind' on the album was an acoustic rendition. The track was originally demoed when *Adrenalize* was being recorded. Next up, 'Two Steps Behind' was banged out in under two hours by the guitarists. Joe then laid the vocals down the next day. When the producers of *The Last Action Hero* came asking for tracks, Leppard gave them a batch of songs. They fell in love with 'Two Steps . . .' but asked if the musical director, Michael Kamen, could put strings on it. Leppard weren't quite sure about this but let him go ahead with the plan after some consultation. Kamen was the brains behind the arrangements on Metallica's 'Nothing Else Matters' and Queensryche's 'Silent Lucidity'. Phil Collen was despatched to keep an eye on Kamen, but he needn't have bothered as the final results were an incredible improvement. With time running out Mike Shipley, who was in LA, anyway, mixed the track in double-quick time. So good was the track that it was released as a single in early September and stormed the charts on both sides of the Atlantic.

Again from the *Hysteria* era was 'She's Too Tough'. Joe wrote the track in approximately fifteen minutes just to pass time in his hotel room in Holland. After demoing the song himself he passed it on to his publishers who in turn passed it on to Canadian rock band Helix. They liked it so much that they used it on their *Wild In The Streets* album in 1987. This was another track that came to light at the end of the *Adrenalize* sessions and again, Phil, Rick Savage, and Rick went in and did their thing while Joe's original vocal from 1985 was kept on the finished product.

Another track which was recorded by another artist was 'Miss You In A Heartbeat'. Phil had written the song but the first recording was by a new band put together by former Free/Bad Company vocalist Paul Rogers called The Law. The version Def Leppard used came about from Joe tinkering around on the piano. He was playing The Beatles' 'Let It Be' when he segued into 'Miss You . . .'. Phil, who had been in the kitchen, implored Joe to record the track, so once again an impromptu recording session was arranged, this one on 22nd April 1992, just two days after the Freddie Mercury gig. The recording then sat on the shelf until the band started putting *Retro Active* together. As the band added their pieces the song grew into the monster track it has since become. For the electric version, which appears later on the album, the guitars were cranked up and the band let rip in what they affectionately call the 'Guitarfest mix'.

The most sobering track on the album, though not musically, was the cover of Mick Ronson's 'Only After Dark'. With Mick receiving chemotherapy treatment for his cancer his funds had dwindled. To help their friend through this financial predicament Ian Hunter, David Bowie, and John Mellencamp, together with Joe, set up a trust fund to pay for his medication. The best way Joe could come up with to earn some hard cash was to cover one of Mick's songs. The band agreed to Joe's request and recorded the song in April 1992 before they set off for tour rehearsals in Ibiza. The track was released as a B-side to 'Let's Get Rocked' with all royalties going to Mick's fund. Unfortunately, when the song came up to be renewed some of the guitar parts had somehow been erased. This enabled Vivian Campbell to get in on the Def Leppard recording act at last. While in Munich the Irishman filled in the missing guitar parts.

'Ride Into The Sun' had been one of the first tracks Def Leppard had ever recorded, appearing initially on their 1978 EP. Later it was recorded for the *Hysteria* B-sides because Phil had heard Sav tinkering with the riff and was blown away by it. The latest version has a much meatier sound along with slightly changed lyrics as Joe was embarrassed to hear the originals which pertained to motorbiking. The new version was modified with a car in mind which was far more suitable to the more mature, car-owning Def Leppard. As neither Phil nor Rick got to play on the original this remix was redone mainly for their benefit. The track also features some wicked honky-tonk piano which was credited secretively to 'The Honky Tonk Messiah'. In actual fact this was Ian Hunter.

The sight of the junkies and down-and-outs on the streets of Dublin inspired Joe to pen 'From The Inside'. Written in 1988 it was premièred on a late-night Irish TV show called *The Dome*, which paired artists with performers from a different musical genre. Having agreed to appear Joe called up Hothouse Flower Liam O'Maonlai who agreed to the performance too. Joe sang with an acoustic guitar while O'Maonlai accompanied him on piano. The version heard on *Retro Active* was recorded during the *Adrenalize* sessions when the Hothouse Flowers partook of a late-night rave at Joe's. Having played it live with them on a couple of occasions before, the Flowers were no strangers to the track and gave it the performance it deserved on its first recording.

'Ring of Fire' got proceedings back to a real rocky edge. This, too, was scheduled to become part of the *Hysteria* album. When two tracks, 'Armageddon It' and 'Pour Some Sugar On Me', came into the reckoning at the death, 'Ring Of Fire' was squeezed out only to be used as the B-side to 'Armageddon It' when it was released as a single in March 1988. With the original version of 'I Wanna Be Your Hero' still requiring much work, the title was pinched for another track which made the album. The song was finally finished with a new intro and chorus during the B-sides sessions for the *Hysteria* singles.

The final track, bar the sneaky addition, was the electric version of 'Two Steps Behind'. It was also recorded in Dublin between the European and Japanese dates of the last tour. The band had been messing with an electric version since April 1992, but had run out of time before they had to retreat to Ibiza to rehearse. While trawling through the tapes of those sessions an unused guitar solo was found which Vivian had, apparently, executed but couldn't remember doing. Being too good to waste the solo was added along with contributions from the rest of the band and the song and album was finished. Steve Clark had writing credits on four of the tracks.

Of course, digging through the old tapes was quite an emotional time for the band. To be heard on the original demos was the sound of Steve discussing the tracks, and the barely audible sound of him puffing on his cigarette. An eerie occurrence but one the band looked on with a fair amount of humour as the tapes brought back many good memories, rather than just the later sad ones. Besides, the songs were of such good quality that it would have been a real shame not to use them. It was an ideal way to remember the former guitarist.

Rick also found that re-recording the tracks gave him an uplift and added to his confidence. A lot of the tracks had originally been recorded not too long after he had lost his arm, the others he had done before the accident. The making of *Retro Active* gave him the opportunity to gauge just how far he had come in his rehabilitation. He said later that: 'It was my chance to pat myself on the back. When I went in and redid the drums it was a breath of fresh air to realize that I'd actually improved quite a lot.' One of the problems encountered by the drummer involved the acoustic tracks and the problem was that Rick is reliant on an electric drum kit. But this they accomplished by beefing up the rest of the sound.

Recording the album out on the road had given *Retro Active* an undeniable edge. Joe put this down, firstly, to the fact that the band wanted to get back to their roots and, secondly, that as they weren't shut away in a studio they were being influenced more by what was going on around them. The reviews for *Retro Active* welcomed this new straight-down-the-wire approach. Much of the speculation centred on the fact that when bands release previously unheard tracks, they were usually not worth being included on albums in the first place. But Def Leppard were the antithesis to that norm. In general the press reviews were very positive.

Also released at the same time as *Retro Active* was a video entitled *Visualize*. The video plotted the past couple of years from pre-*Adrenalize* days to the present. As well as the *Adrenalize* videos the ninety-minute film included the clips of their guest appearances with Ben E. King for a rendition of 'Stand By Me' and a late-night TV programme where Joe got up with the Hothouse Flowers and Rolling Stone Ronnie Wood for a jam. There were also various interviews, but the heartrending moment was the tribute to Steve which took the form of a montage of shots set against the musical backdrop of the instrumental from *High 'n' Dry*, 'Switch 625'.

With the 'Adrenalize' tour over and *Retro Active* released it was time to wind down, time to go home and put the feet up. Contrary to belief, not all the band members were happy to see the end of the tour. Joe, having been unhappy at the elongated 'Hysteria' tour, would have been more than happy to carry on. Even though he was happy to see the back of that particular tour, after a few weeks at home he was bouncing off the walls, so what would this break bring him now he was up for a few more gigs? Vivian was, of course, keen to start the next album. In his previous bands he had been presided over by domineering vocalists, so this would be his opportunity to ensconce himself fully by contributing to the writing process. Rick and Phil were heading home to their houses in Los Angeles where they'd now relocated. Phil was eager to get home to spend more time with his son Rory who was now four years of age. Rick just wanted the rest and to reacquaint himself with his place in the LA suburbs of Studio City.

Out of all the band members Sav was the most eager to get off the road. He had contracted tendonitis in a finger which had made the last leg of the tour very painful for him. At the end he could hardly hold a plectrum let alone pluck with any serious conviction. His home in Dublin beckoned, and not before time.

Sav was also planning to tie the knot with his long-time partner Dara Corcoran. The wedding would take place before the year was out in Clontarf, near Dublin.

Before leaving the arenas in their wake for the foreseeable future, the band were still answering criticisms that they used backing tapes to beef up their sound and cover their own shortcomings. Rick, it was alleged, was making much use of the technology afforded to him. Leppard countered that the kit possessed many triggers and samples which Rick actually had to play which keeps them 'live'. On any other queries on masking the roots of their sound, the band would counteract by insisting these accusations were totally false and that maybe the sound they achieved on stage was so good because they rehearsed and prepared for their tours much harder than anyone else.

The future moves of Def Leppard seem a little shrouded as to what form the next album would take. All were agreed that writing for the album would definitely begin before the end of 1993. The major question was how they would set about recording their sixth studio album. Phil had stated unequivocally that the process of recording *Retro Active* had 'taken a stick out of their ass'. As to the technique they had previously enjoyed, whether Mutt Lange would be behind the console was open to debate. Early signs were that he would be retained in a song-writing capacity, but production duties would have to be decided when the recording began. With the addition of Vivian to the writing fold, the consensus of opinion is that Leppard would undoubtedly deviate from the path that had been well trodden up to this point.

Def Leppard have enjoyed enormous success on a scale far beyond any of their wildest schoolboy expectations. But that success has come at an immense personal and emotional cost, not the least of which was the tragic death of Steve Clark. But, like mountaineers who continue to risk their lives for the thrill of scaling new peaks, Joe, Sav, Rick, Phil, and Vivian will carry on performing rock 'n' roll, climbing, and conquering, their own kinds of peak. There is still more to come . . .

CHAPTER SIXTEEN

THE SONG REMAINS THE SAME

– THE DEF LEPPARD DISCOGRAPHY

The Def Leppard discography (UK releases only)

There is some confusion over the original Def Leppard EP, *Getcha Rocks Off*, there being two pressings printed with two different coloured labels, but with both versions being issued on the band's own Bludgeon Riffola Records. The unsold copies were subsequently picked up by Phonogram Records at the time the band were signed and then re-issued under a *third* catalogue number. Hopefully this will clear up any lingering doubts.

SINGLES
Bludgeon Riffola releases:

'Ride Into The Sun' / 'Getcha Rocks Off' / 'Overture'

Release date: January 1979

SRTS/78/CUS 232 (Pressed with red label. First 500 with lyric sheet enclosed)

'Ride Into The Sun' / 'Getcha Rocks Off' / 'Overture'

Release date: May 1979

MSB 001 (pressed with yellow label)

Vertigo releases:

'Getcha Rocks Off' / 'Ride Into   6059 240
The Sun' / 'Overture'
   Release date: September 1979

'Wasted' / 'Hello America'   6059 247
   Release date: 17th November 1979

'Hello America' / 'Good Morning   LEPP 1
Freedom'
   Release date: 21st February 1980

'Let it Go' / 'Switch 625'   LEPP 2 (First 10,000 issued in
                                       picture sleeve with patch)

   Release date: August 1981

'Bringin' On The Heartbreak' /   LEPP 3
'Me And My Wine'
   Release date: 13th November 1981

'Bringin' On The Heartbreak' /   LEPP 312 (12″ single with
'Me And My Wine' / 'You Got   different sleeve design)
Me Runnin''
   Release date: 13th November 1981

'Photograph' / 'Bringin' On the   VER 5
Heartbreak'
   Release date: 3rd February 1983

'Photograph' / 'Bringin' On the   VERP 5 (500 only limited
Heartbreak'   edition 'pop-up' camera picture
                                       bag)
   Release date: 3rd February 1983

'Photograph' / 'Bringin' On the
Heartbreak'

VERQ 5 (special edition of
VERP 5 with different insert
photo of Marilyn Monroe)

Release date: 3rd February 1983

'Photograph' / 'Bringin' On the
Heartbreak' / 'Mirror Mirror'

VERX 5 (12″ single)

Release date: 3rd February 1983

'Rock of Ages' / 'Action Not
Words'

VER 6

Release date: 20th May 1983

'Rock of Ages' / 'Action Not
Words'

VERP 6 (picture disc of black
Ibanez guitar)

Release date: 20th May 1983

'Rock of Ages' / 'Action Not
Words'

VERQ 6 (limited edition fold-
out 'Rock box')

Release date: 20th May 1983

'Too Late' / 'Foolin''

VER 8

Release date: 25th November 1983

'Too Late' / 'Foolin'' / 'High 'n'
Dry (Saturday Night)'

VERX 8 (12″ single)

Release date: 25th November 1983

'Photograph' / 'Bringin' On the
Heartbreak'

VER 9 (re-issue with different
sleeve)

Release date: 17th February 1984

'Photograph' / 'Bringin' On The
Heartbreak' / 'Mirror Mirror
(Look Into My Eyes)'
    Release date: 17th Febraury 1984

VERX 9 (12″ single, re-issue)

'Photograph' / 'Bringin' On The
Heartbreak'
    Release date: 17th February 1984

VERG 9 (limited edition
gatefold wallet cover)

'Bringin' On The Heartbreak'
(Remix) / 'Me And My Wine'
(Remix)
    Release date: 1984

VERX 10 (12″ single)

'Animal' / 'Tear It Down'
    Release date: 20th July 1987

LEP 1

'Animal' (Extended mix) /
'Animal' / 'Tear It Down'
    Release date: 20th July 1987

LEPX 1 (12″ single)

'Animal' (Extended mix) /
'Animal' / 'Tear It Down' /
'Women'
    Release date: 20th July 1987

LEPMC 1 (cassette single)

'Animal' (Extended mix) /
'Animal' / 'Tear It Down' /
'Women'
    Release date: 20th July 1987

LEPCD (limited edition CD
single, 3000 only, numbered)

'Animal' / 'Animal' (Extended
mix) / 'Tear It Down'
    Release date: July 1987

LEPC 1 (limited edition red
vinyl, not commercially available)

'Pour Some Sugar On Me' / 'I   LEP 2
Wanna Be Your Hero'
    Release date: 14th September 1987

'Pour Some Sugar On Me' / 'I   LEPS 2 (limited edition triangle
Wanna Be Your Hero'   shaped picture disc in 12″ silver
                                  gatefold cover)
    Release date: 14th September 1987

'Pour Some Sugar On Me' / 'I   LEPMC 2 (cassette single)
Wanna Be Your Hero'
    Release date: 14th September 1987

'Pour Some Sugar On Me'   LEPX 2 (12″ single in silver
(Extended mix) / 'Pour Some   gatefold sleeve)
Sugar On Me' / 'I Wanna Be
Your Hero'
    Release date: 14th September 1987

'Pour Some Sugar On Me'   LEPPX 2 (12″ picture disc)
(Extended mix) / 'Pour Some
Sugar On Me' / 'I Wanna Be
Your Hero'
    Release date: 14th September 1987

'Hysteria' / 'Ride Into The Sun'   LEP 3
(Remake)
    Release date: 23rd November 1987

'Hysteria' / 'Ride Into The Sun'   LEPS 3 (limited edition with
(Remake)   patch)
    Release date: 30th November 1987

'Hysteria' / 'Ride Into The Sun'   LEPX 3
(Remake) / 'Love & Affection'
(Live)
    Release date: 23rd November 1987

'Hysteria' / 'Ride Into The Sun'   LEPX 313 (limited edition in
(Remake) / 'Love & Affection'   envelope sleeve with poster &
(Live)   discography)
    Release date: 30th November 1987

'Hysteria' / 'Ride Into The Sun'   LEPMC 3 (cassette single)
(Remake) / 'Love & Affection'
(Live)/ 'I Wanna Be Your Hero'
    Release date: 23rd November 1987

'Hysteria' / 'Ride Into The Sun'   LEPCD 3 (CD single, normal
(Remake) / 'Love & Affection'   edition with titles in yellow ink &
(Live) / 'I Wanna Be Your Hero'   rest in red)
    Release date: 23rd November 1987

'Hysteria' / 'Ride Into The Sun'   LEPCD 3 (limited edition CD
(Remake) / 'Love & Affection'   single, 1000 only numbered,
(Live) / 'I Wanna Be Your Hero'   with titles in red ink & rest in
                                          yellow)
    Release date: 23rd November 1987

'Armageddon It' (Atomic mix) /   LEP 4
'Ring Of Fire'
    Release date: March 1988

'Armageddon It' (Atomic mix) /   LEPP 4 (limited edition
'Ring Of Fire'   posterbag)
    Release date: March 1988

'Armageddon It' / 'Armageddon
It' (Atomic mix) / 'Ring Of Fire'
Release date: March 1988

LEPX 4 (12″ single)

'Armageddon It' / 'Armageddon
It' (Atomic mix) / 'Ring Of Fire'

LEPX B4 (limited edition boxed
set, 5000 numbered copies with
poster, enamel badge & 5
postcards)

Release date: March 1988

'Armageddon It'/ 'Armageddon
It' (Atomic mix) /
Release date: March 1988

LEPCD 4 (limited edition CD
picture disc)

'Love Bites' / 'Billy's Got A Gun'
(Live)
Release date: May 1988

LEP 5

'Love Bites' / 'Billy's Got A Gun'
(Live)
Release date: May 1988

LEPDJ 5 (promo issue with
radio edit A-side)

'Love Bites' / 'Billy's Got A Gun'
(Live)
Release date: May 1988

LEPG 5 (limited edition
numbered gatefold lyric book)

'Love Bites' / 'Billy's Got A Gun'
(Live) / 'Excitable' (Orgasmic mix)
Release date: May 1988

LEPX 5 (12″ single)

'Love Bites' / 'Rocket' (Lunar
mix) / 'Billy's Got A Gun' (Live)
Release date: May 1988

LEPCD 5 (CD single)

'Love Bites' / 'Billy's Got A Gun' (live) / 'Excitable' (Orgasmic mix)

    Release date: May 1988

LEPX B5 (Boxed set with 4 'Hysteria' cardboard printed squares)

'Rocket' / 'Release me'
    Release date: 30th January 1989

LEP 6

'Rocket' / 'Release me'
    Release date: 30th January 1989

LEPC 6 (special 'Brit Pack' box)

'Rocket' (Lunar mix) / 'Release me' / 'Rock Of Ages' (Live)
    Release date: 30th January 1989

LEPX 6 (12″ single)

'Rocket' (Lunar mix) / 'Rocket' (Radio edit) / 'Release Me'

    Release date: 30th January 1989

LEPX P6 (limited edition 12″ picture disc, 3500 only individually numbered on disc)

'Let's Get Rocked' / 'Only After Dark'
    Release date: 23rd March 1992

DEF 7

'Let's Get Rocked' / 'Only After Dark'
    Release date: 23rd March 1992

DEFX P7 (12″ single)

'Let's Get Rocked' / 'Only After Dark'
    Release date: 23rd March 1992

DEFMC 7 (cassette single)

'Let's Get Rocked' / 'Only After Dark' / 'Woman' (Live)
    Release date: 23rd March 1992

DEFCD 7 (CD single)

'Make Love Like A Man' / 'Miss   LEP 7
You In A Heartbeat'
    Release date: June 1992

'Have You Ever Needed   LEP 8
Someone So Bad' / 'From The
Inside'
    Release date: 1st September 1993

'Have You Ever Needed   LEPXP 8 (12″ picture disc)
Someone So Bad' / 'From The
Inside' / 'You Can't Always Get
What You Want'
    Release date: 1st September 1993

'Heaven Is' / 'She's Too Tough'   LEP 9 (special edition
                                     autographed etched disc)
    Release date: 18th January 1993

'Heaven Is' / 'She's Too Tough' /   LEPMC 9 (cassette single)
'Elected' (Live) / 'Let's Get
Rocked' (Live)
    Release date: 18th January 1993

'Heaven Is' / 'She's Too Tough' /   LEPCD 9 (CD single)
'Elected' (Live) / 'Let's Get
Rocked' (Live)
    Release date: 18th January 1993

'Tonight' / 'Now I'm Here'   LEP 10
(Live)
    Release date: 19th April 1993

'Tonight' / 'Now I'm Here' (Live) / 'Photograph' (Live) 　　Release date: 19th April 1993	LEPMC 10 (cassette single)
'Tonight' / 'Now I'm Here' (Live) / 'Photograph' (Live) 　　Release date: 19th April 1993	LEPCD 10 (CD single)
'Two Steps Behind' / 'Tonight' (Acoustic version) / 'S.M.C.' 　　Release date: September 1993	LEP 12
'Action' / 'She's Too Tough' (Joe's demo) / 'Miss You In A Heartbeat' (Phil's demo) 　　Release date: 4th January 1994	LEP 13
'Action' / 'She's Too Tough' (Joe's demo) / 'Miss You In A Heartbeat' (Phil's demo) 　　Release date: 4th January 1994	LLEP 13 (limited edition CD single with discography)

Stumpus Maximus & The Gold Ol' Boys
'Release Me' / 'Rock Of Ages' (Live – by Def Leppard)
　　Release date: January 1989

LEPDK 6 (limited edition promo 12" single, rumoured to be only 1000 pressed)

ALBUMS
Vertigo releases:

On Through the Night   6360 180

'Rock Brigade' / 'Hello America' /
'Sorrow Is A Woman' / 'It Could
Be You' / 'Satellite' / 'When The
Walls Come Tumblin' Down' /
'Wasted' / 'Rocks Off' / 'It Don't
Matter' / 'Answer To The
Master' / 'Overture'
   Release date: 14th March 1980

High 'n' Dry   6359 045

'Let It Go' / 'Another Hit And
Run' / 'High 'n' Dry (Saturday
Night)' / 'Bringin' On The
Heartbreak' / 'Switch 625' / 'You
Got Me Runnin'' / 'Lady Strange'
/ 'On Through The Night' /
'Mirror Mirror (Look Into My
Eyes)' / 'No No No'
   Release date: July 1981

Pyromania   VERS 2

'Rock! Rock! (Till You Drop)' /
'Photograph' / 'Stagefright' /
'Too Late For Love' / 'Die Hard
The Hunter' / 'Foolin'' / 'Rock
Of Ages' / 'Comin' Under Fire' /
'Action! Not Words!' / 'Billy's
Got A Gun'
   Release date: February 1983

Bludgeon Riffola releases:

Hysteria

HYSLP 1

'Women' / 'Rocket' / 'Animal' /
'Love Bites' / 'Pour Some Sugar
On Me' / 'Armageddon It' /
'Gods Of War' / 'Don't Shoot
Shotgun' / 'Run Riot' / 'Hysteria'
/ 'Excitable' / 'Love And
Affection'
    Release date: 3rd August 1987

Hysteria

HYSPD 1 (limited edition
picture disc)

    Release date: 3rd August 1987

Adrenalize

510978 1

'Let's Get Rocked' / 'Heaven Is' /
'Make Love Like A Man' /
'Tonight' / 'White Lightning' /
'Stand Up' / 'Kick Love Into
Motion' / 'Personal Property' /
'Have You Ever Needed
Someone So Bad' / 'I Wanna
Touch U' / 'Tear It Down'
    Release date: 30th March 1992

Adrenalize

514256 1 (limited edition picture
disc)

    Release date: December 1992

Retro Active

518305 1

'Desert Song' / 'Fractured Love' /
'Action' / 'Two Steps Behind'
(Acoustic version) / 'She's Too
Tough' / 'Miss You In A
Heartbeat' / 'Only After Dark' /
'Ride Into The Sun' / 'From The
Inside' / 'Ring Of Fire' / 'I Wanna
Be Your Hero' / 'Miss You In A
Heartbeat' (Electric version) /
'Two Steps Behind' (Electric
version)

Release date: 4th October 1993

VIDEOS
Polygram Music releases:

Historia

CFV 07892

'Hello America' / 'Let It Go' /
'High'n'Dry / 'Bringin' On The
Heartbreak' (Version 1 w/Pete
Willis) / 'Photograph' / 'Rock Of
Ages' / 'Foolin'' / 'Too Late For
Love' / 'Rock! Rock! (Till You
Drop)' / 'Bringin' On The
Heartbreak' (Version 2 w/ Phil
Collen) / 'Me And My Wine' /
'Women' / 'Animal' / 'Pour Some
Sugar On Me' (UK version) /
'Hysteria' / 'Armageddon It'
(Live version) / 'Pour Some
Sugar On Me' (US live version)

Release date: 1988

Live In The Round In Your Face

CFV 08422

'Stagefright' / 'Rock! Rock! (Till You Drop)' / 'Women' / 'Too Late For Love' / 'Hysteria' / 'Gods Of War' / 'Die Hard The Hunter' / 'Bringin' On The Heartbreak' / 'Foolin'' / 'Armageddon It' / 'Animal' / 'Pour Some Sugar On Me' / 'Rock Of Ages' / 'Photograph'
    Release date: 1989

Visualize

086 506–3

Opening Statements And Titles / 'Rocket' / 'Switch 625' (Steve Clark Tribute) / 'Solo Projects/ Making Videos / 'Let's Get Rocked' / 'Vivian Campbell Joins Def Leppard / 'Make Love Like A Man' / 'I Wanna Touch U' / 'Have You Ever Needed Someone So Bad' / Interviews / 'Tonight' / 'Heaven Is' / Fans/Off Stage Life / 'Stand Up (Kick Love Into Motion)' / Return To Sheffield / 'Two Steps Behind' (Live From Sheffield) / 'Photograph' (Live From Sheffield) / The Future Of Def Leppard
    Release date: October 1993

INDEX